THIS BOOK
BELONGS TO

BY
THE SAME
AUTHOR:

The Circle and the Cross
The Song of the Earth

COMPACT DISCS:

The Circle and the Cross with Aisling
The Song of the Earth with Aisling
The Moon on the Lake
with Peter Kennard
The Loom of Music
solo album

All music released
through Movieplay
Australia

WISDOM
FROM THE
CELTIC
TRADITION

SCRATCHES
IN THE
MARGIN

CAISEAL MÓR

If you would like to write to Caiseal Mor, he can be
contacted at the following e-mail address: cais@real.com.au

Random House Australia Pty Ltd
20 Alfred Street, Milsons Point, NSW 2061

Sydney   New York   Toronto
London   Auckland   Johannesburg
and agencies throughout the world

First published 1996

National Library of Australia
Cataloguing-in-Publication Data

Mór Caiseal, 1961- .
  Scratches in the margin.

  ISBN 0 09 183327 2.

  1. Proverbs, Irish - Translations into English. 2. Irish
  poetry - To 1100 - Translations into English. 3. Folklore -
  Ireland. I. Title.

891.6211

Designed by Caiseal Mór
Typeset by Asset Typesetting, Sydney
Printed by Griffin Paperbacks, Adelaide

TO
SELWA

AND ALL THE OTHER
WISE ONES
WHO HAVE
GUIDED ME

ACKNOWLEDGEMENTS

TO EVERYONE WHO HELPED MAKE
THIS BOOK POSSIBLE, ESPECIALLY TO NANCY, MY
PARTNER, WHO HELPED WITH THE LAYOUT.
THANKS TO SELWA, MY AGENT, WHO SAW THE
POTENTIAL OF THIS LITTLE BOOK AND WORKED HARD
TO MAKE IT A REALITY.
AND THANK YOU TO ALL AT
RANDOM HOUSE
FOR GETTING
BEHIND IT.

INTRODUCTION

Some of the lines in this little book were first written down over a thousand years ago. Most of the wisdom is much older than that. Other pieces were collected by Alexander Carmichael in the late nineteenth century on his journeys through the Highlands of Scotland. His book *Carmina Gadelica* is full of pagan survivals and folk charms. The rest I gathered when I was in Ireland ten years ago from old people and self-appointed Senachies or storytellers. Those readers who are familiar with my novels will realise that I have incorporated many of the shorter sayings into my own tales. I find the ancient poems an endless source of inspiration.

The early Christian fathers tolerated the pagan customs of Ireland, in some cases taking on some of the old beliefs. Because of this tolerance a large number of ancient Gaelic legends, poems and wise one-liners were preserved and even incorporated into Christian tales at times. Monasteries were also paid by local chieftains to record their family histories. The monks became very adept at relating the exploits of legendary figures and comparing their adventures to those of a current leader or clan. A good story ensured the patronage of the local nobility.

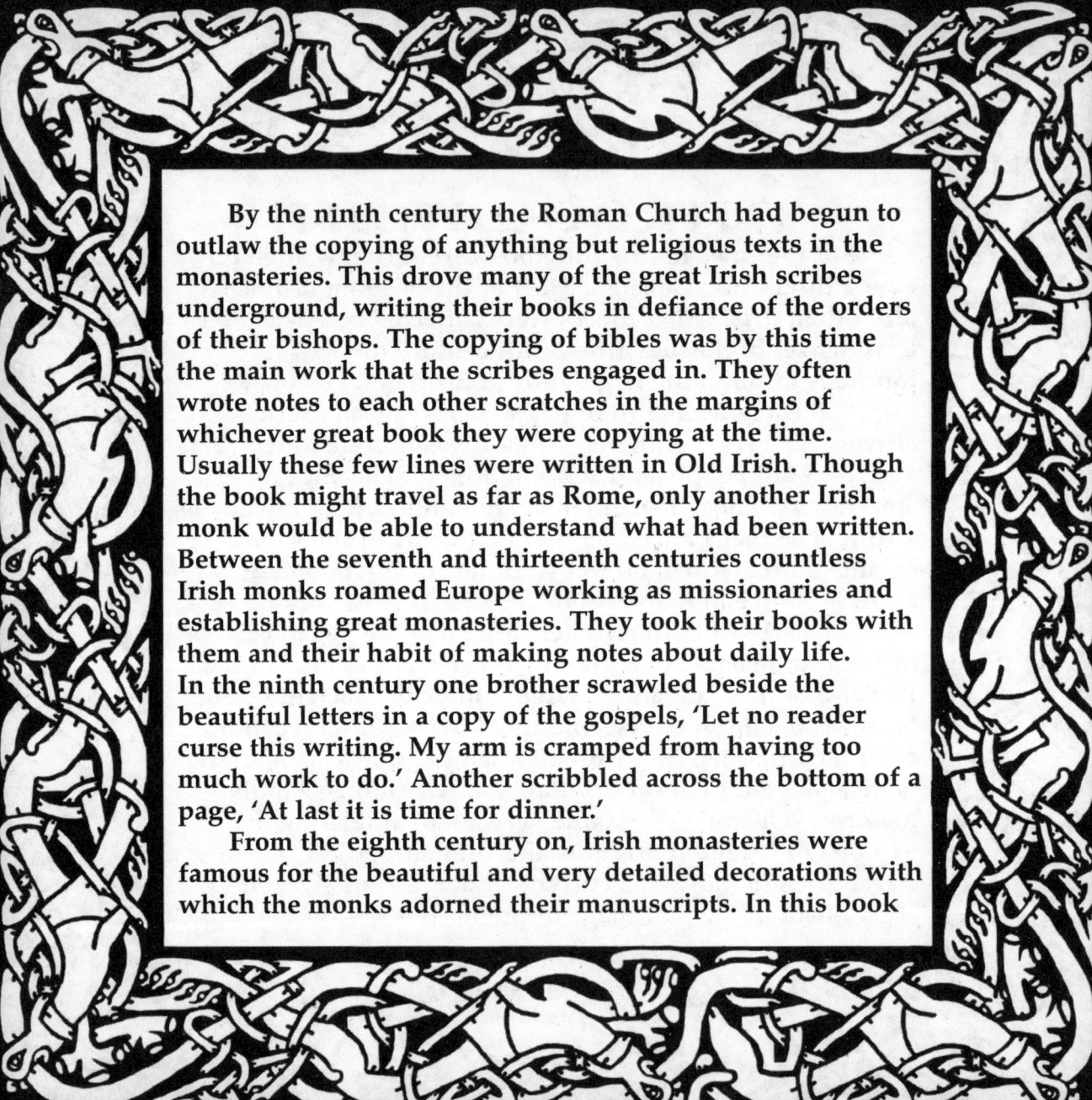

By the ninth century the Roman Church had begun to outlaw the copying of anything but religious texts in the monasteries. This drove many of the great Irish scribes underground, writing their books in defiance of the orders of their bishops. The copying of bibles was by this time the main work that the scribes engaged in. They often wrote notes to each other scratches in the margins of whichever great book they were copying at the time. Usually these few lines were written in Old Irish. Though the book might travel as far as Rome, only another Irish monk would be able to understand what had been written. Between the seventh and thirteenth centuries countless Irish monks roamed Europe working as missionaries and establishing great monasteries. They took their books with them and their habit of making notes about daily life. In the ninth century one brother scrawled beside the beautiful letters in a copy of the gospels, 'Let no reader curse this writing. My arm is cramped from having too much work to do.' Another scribbled across the bottom of a page, 'At last it is time for dinner.'

From the eighth century on, Irish monasteries were famous for the beautiful and very detailed decorations with which the monks adorned their manuscripts. In this book

I have illustrated some of the poems and sayings with pages inspired by the early eighth century *Book of Kells*, with patterns derived from the later *Book of Lindisfarne* and designs that can be still seen on standing stones throughout Ireland and Britain.

I have also included some illustrations that represent the carpet pages of the ancient Gospel books. These highly decorated pages were meant to inspire contemplation and meditation. They were similar in some respects to Hindu and Buddhist mandalas in that the symbols used were understood to help one come closer to the goal of one's meditations and open up the mind to the grace of God.

Above all this book is my tribute to the early Christian monks without whom so many Irish traditions would have been lost forever. Thanks mostly to those nameless brothers, the tales of the ancient days have been preserved and the simple wisdom of the travelling friars can still be appreciated.

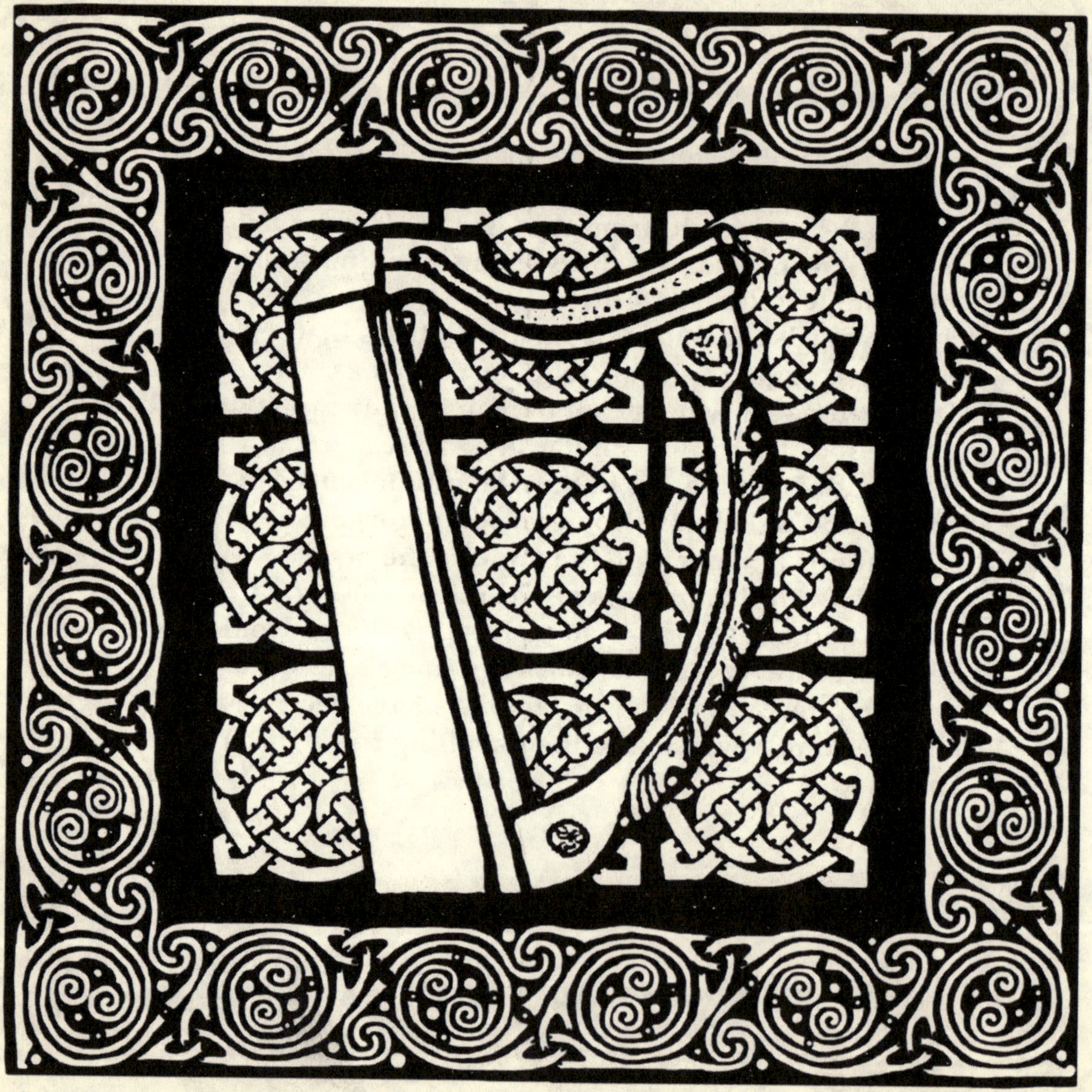

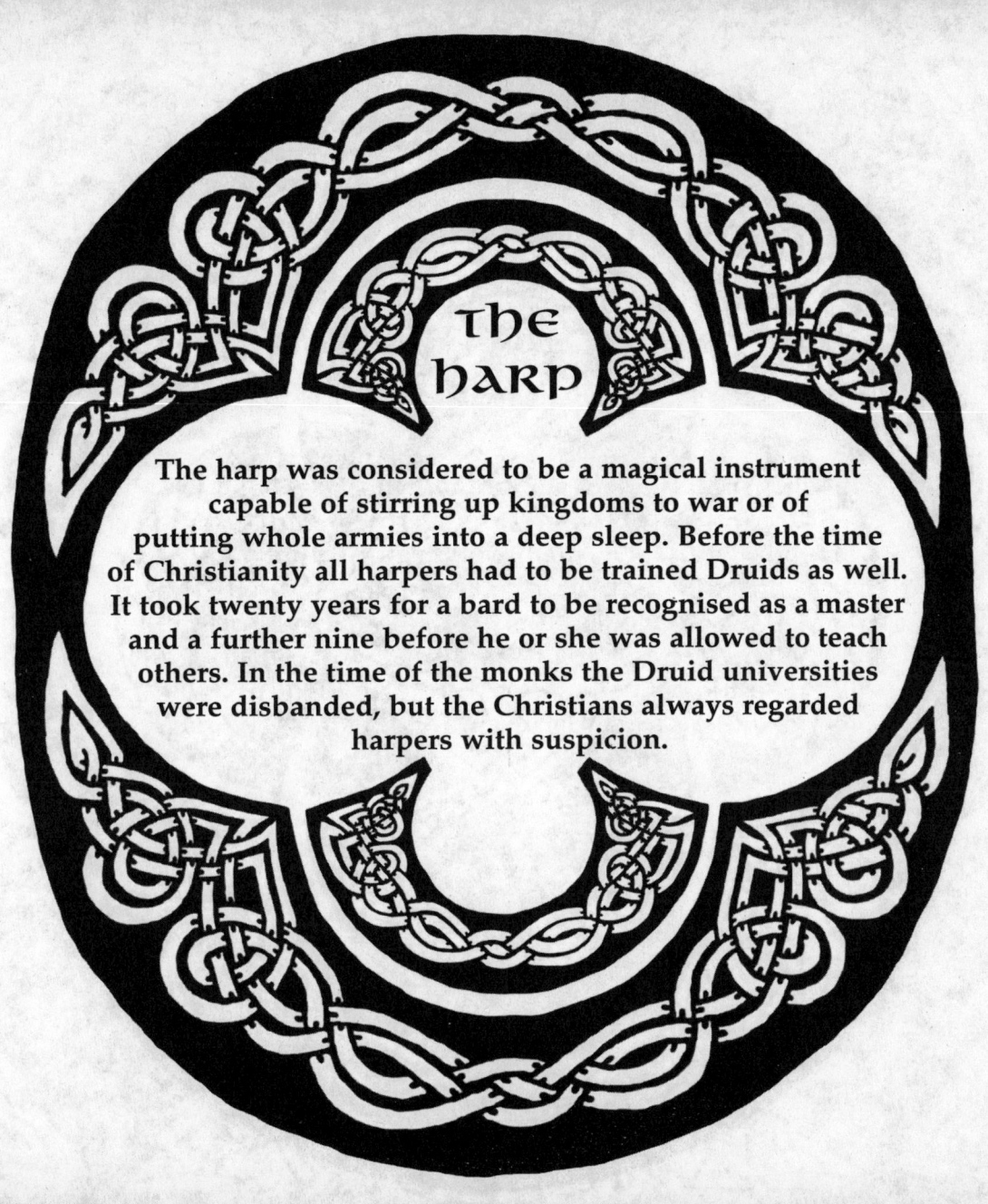

the harp

The harp was considered to be a magical instrument capable of stirring up kingdoms to war or of putting whole armies into a deep sleep. Before the time of Christianity all harpers had to be trained Druids as well. It took twenty years for a bard to be recognised as a master and a further nine before he or she was allowed to teach others. In the time of the monks the Druid universities were disbanded, but the Christians always regarded harpers with suspicion.

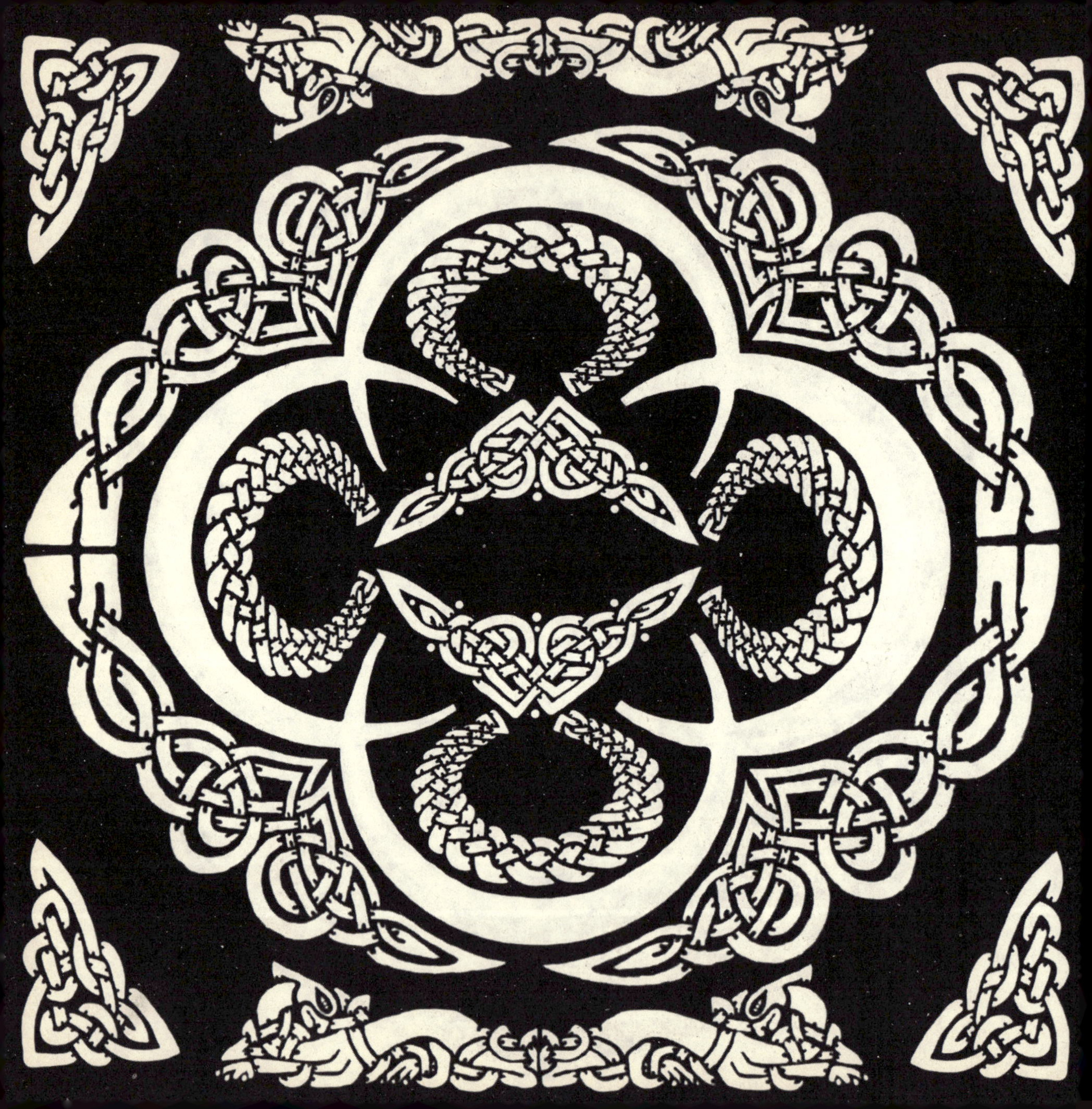

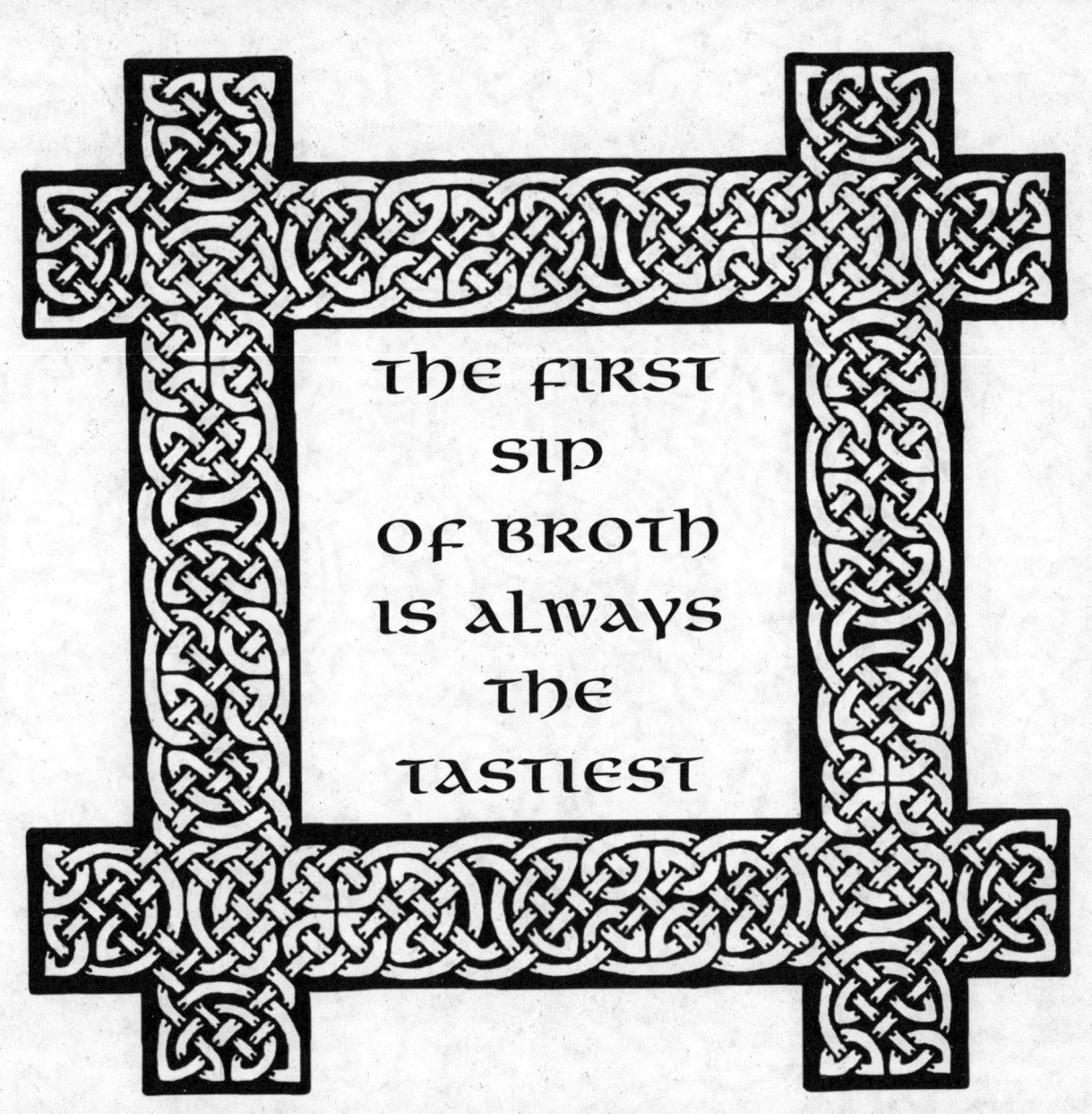

THE FIRST
SIP
OF BROTH
IS ALWAYS
THE
TASTIEST

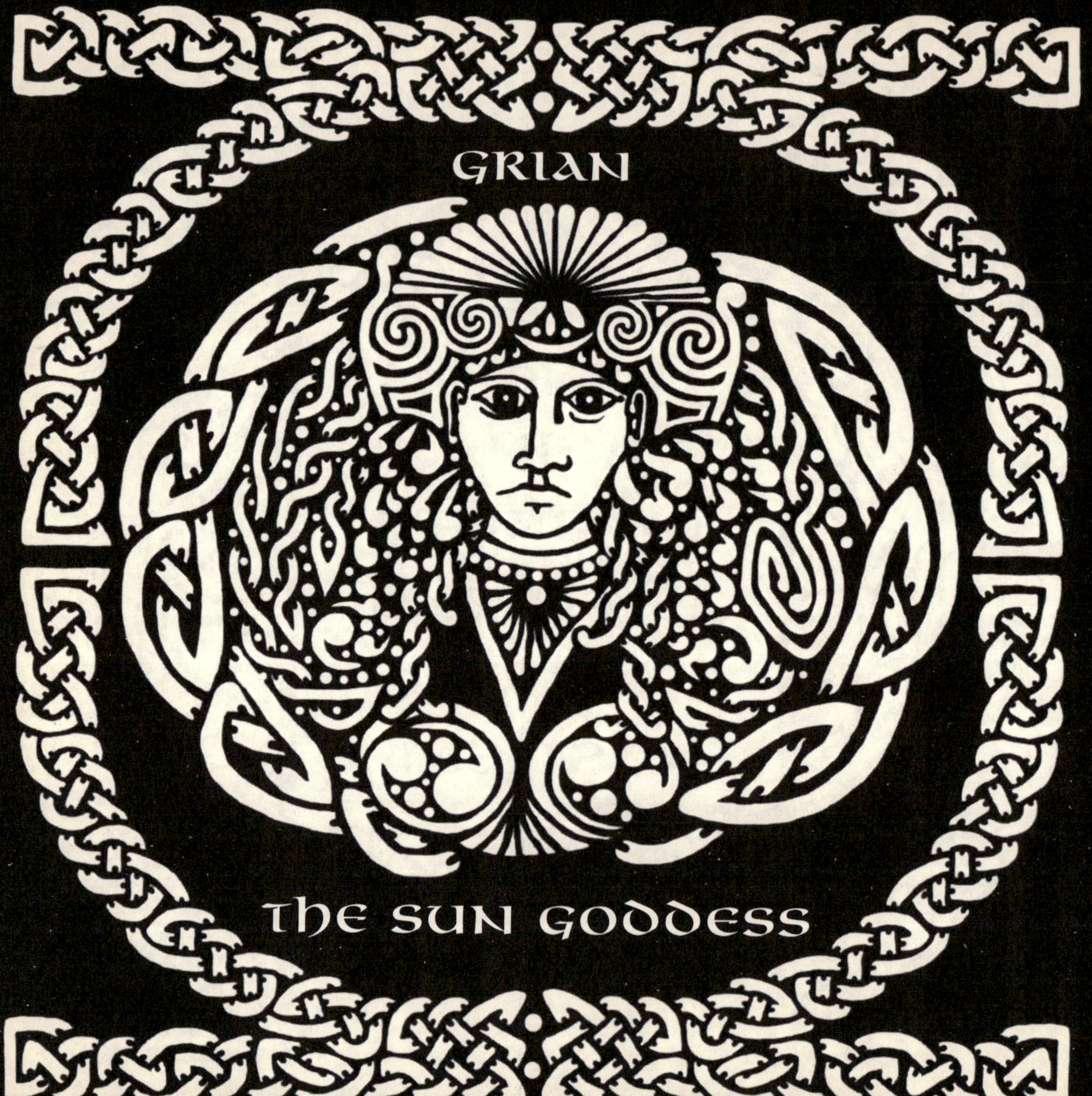
GRIAN
THE SUN GODDESS

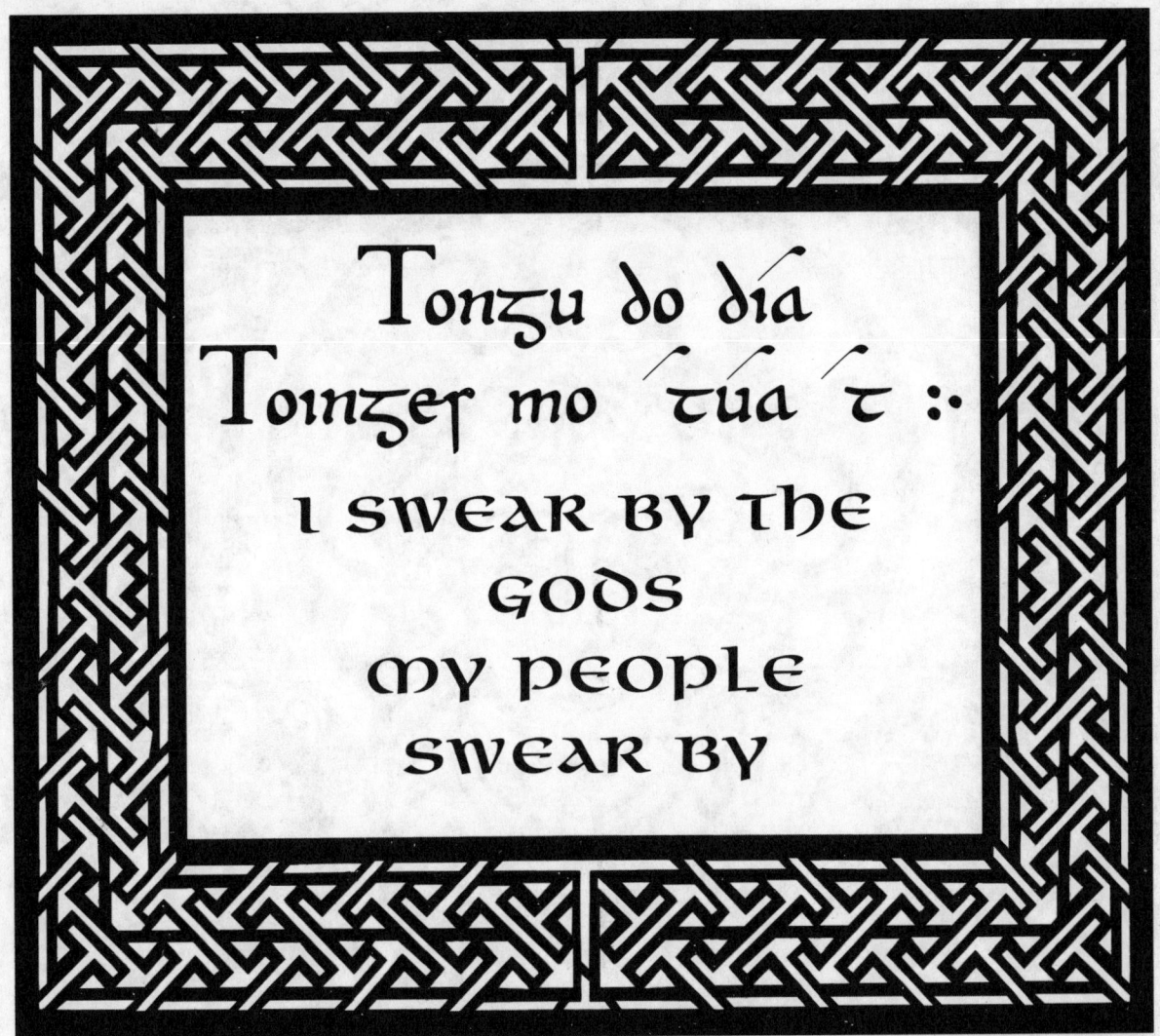

Tongu do día
Toinger mo tuát :.
I SWEAR BY THE
GODS
MY PEOPLE
SWEAR BY

The ancient Celts believed that it was wrong to reveal the names of their Gods to people from outside their immediate tribe. So it was common for their chieftains to swear this oath whenever treaties were agreed.

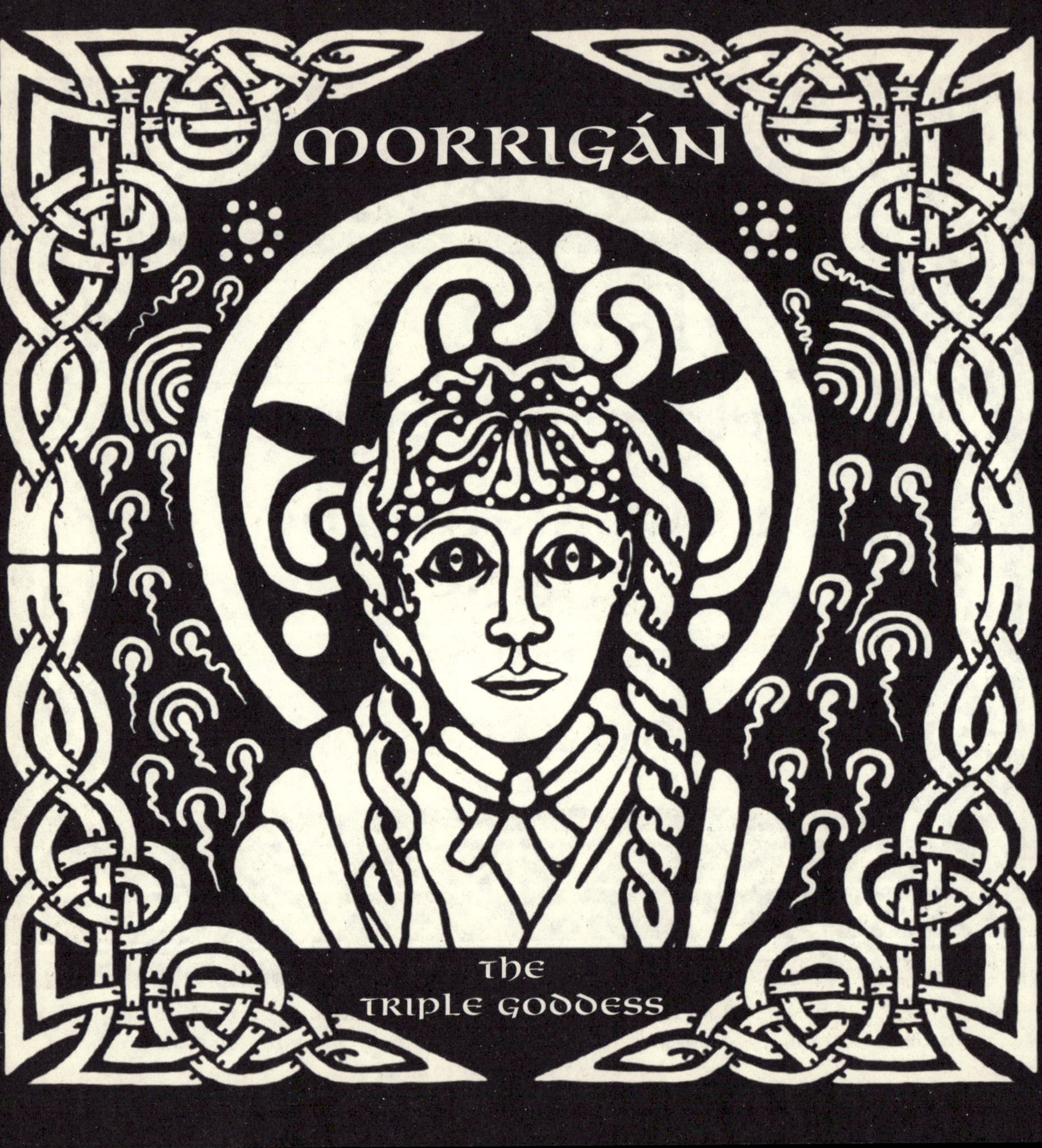
MORRIGÁN
THE
TRIPLE GODDESS

GODS & GODDESSES

The ancient Celtic peoples worshipped many different deities depending on their region of origin. In Ireland before Christianity, the Tuatha-De-Danaan were the chief deities. Their leaders were Dagda the King of Summer and his wife Grian the Sun Goddess. Their rivals were Cailleach the Queen of Winter and her husband Manannan Mac Lir Lord of the Sea, who was often depicted on standing stones as a faceless merman.

Bridgid the Goddess of Fire was most beloved of all the deities. The Christian monks found her so popular that they were forced to convert her to the Cross. So the stories of Saint Bridgid came about. Few who pray to her today realise that she predates Christianity by hundreds of years.

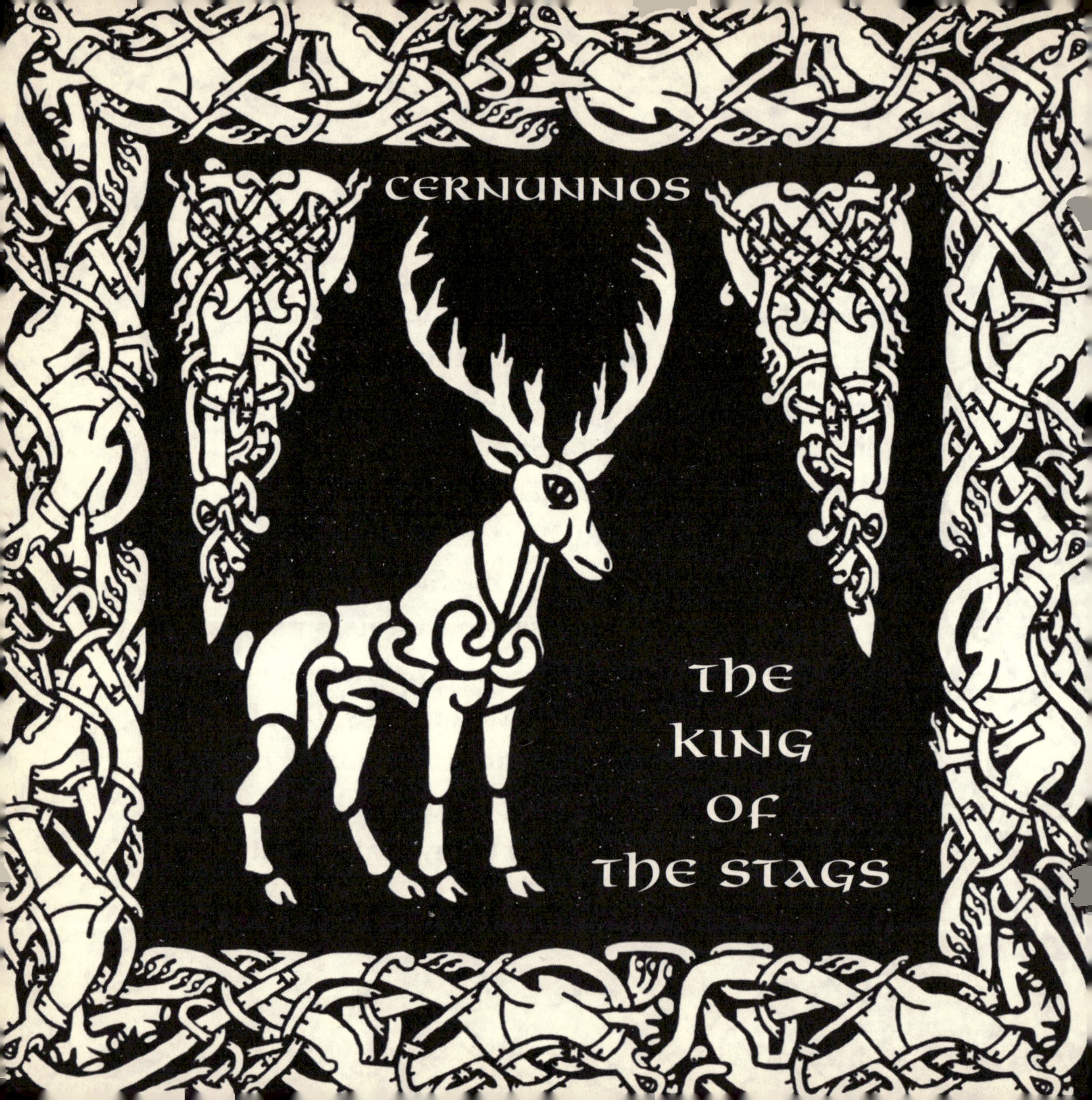
CERNUNNOS
THE KING OF THE STAGS

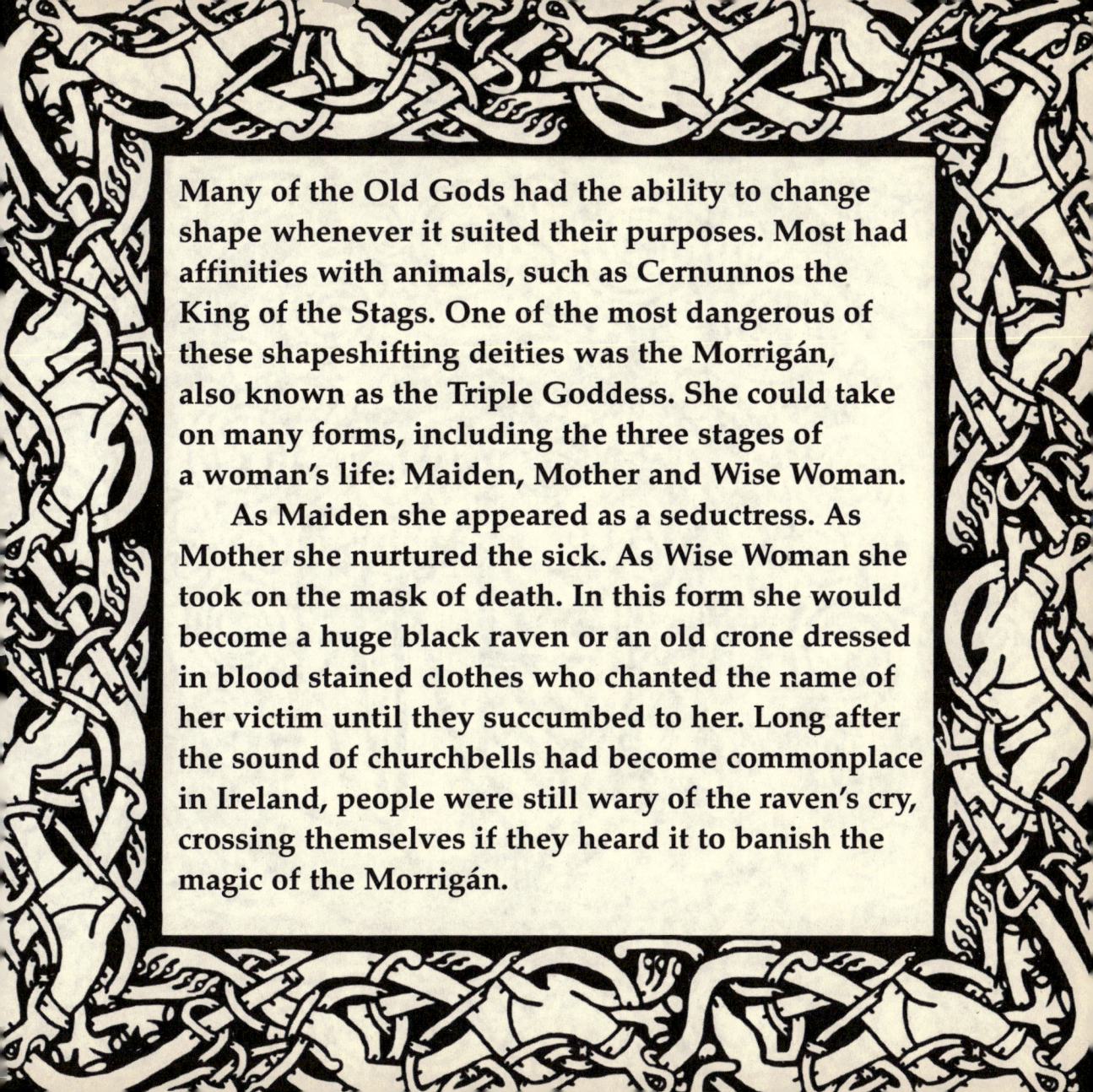

Many of the Old Gods had the ability to change shape whenever it suited their purposes. Most had affinities with animals, such as Cernunnos the King of the Stags. One of the most dangerous of these shapeshifting deities was the Morrigán, also known as the Triple Goddess. She could take on many forms, including the three stages of a woman's life: Maiden, Mother and Wise Woman.

As Maiden she appeared as a seductress. As Mother she nurtured the sick. As Wise Woman she took on the mask of death. In this form she would become a huge black raven or an old crone dressed in blood stained clothes who chanted the name of her victim until they succumbed to her. Long after the sound of churchbells had become commonplace in Ireland, people were still wary of the raven's cry, crossing themselves if they heard it to banish the magic of the Morrigán.

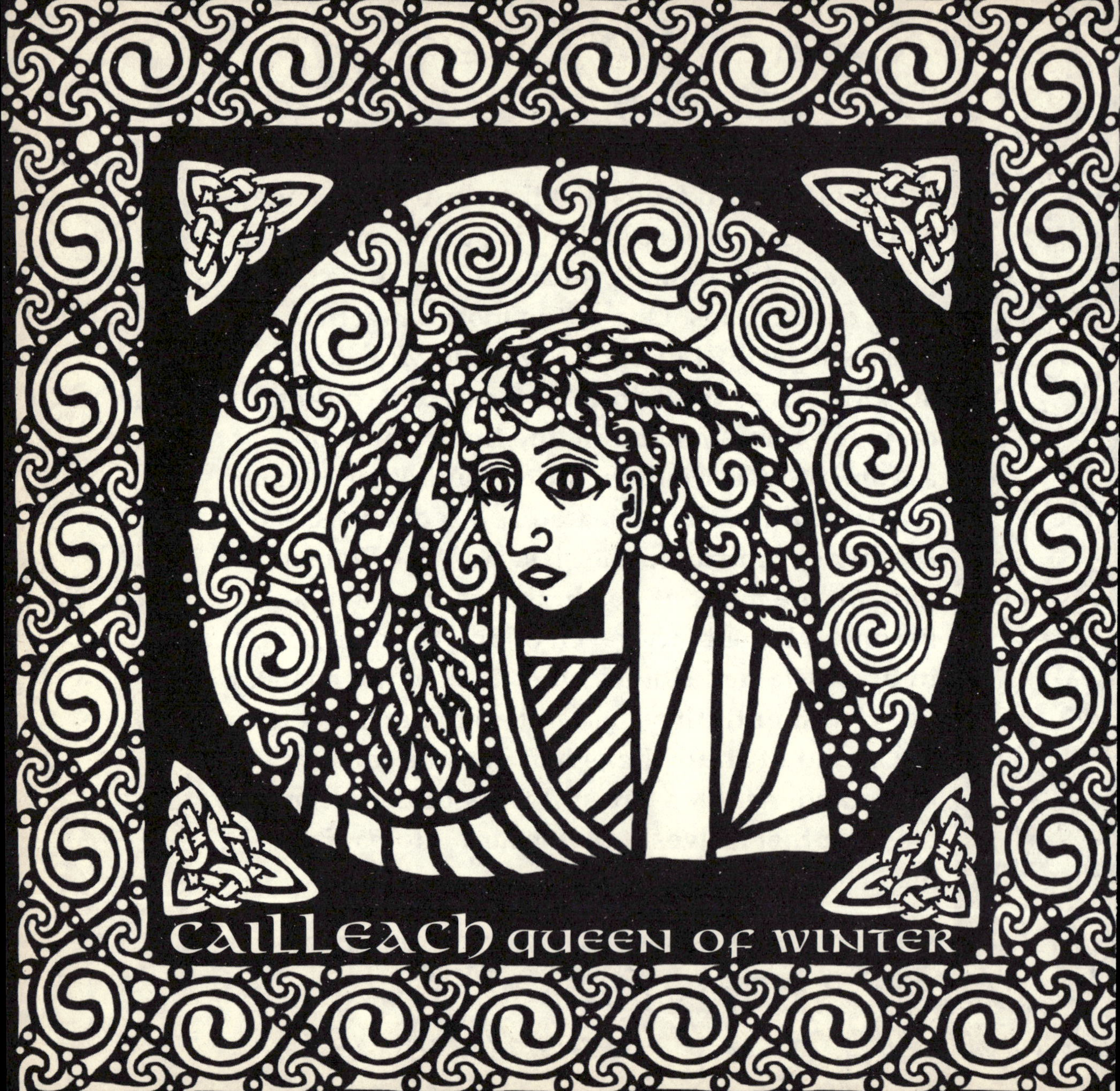
Cailleach Queen of Winter

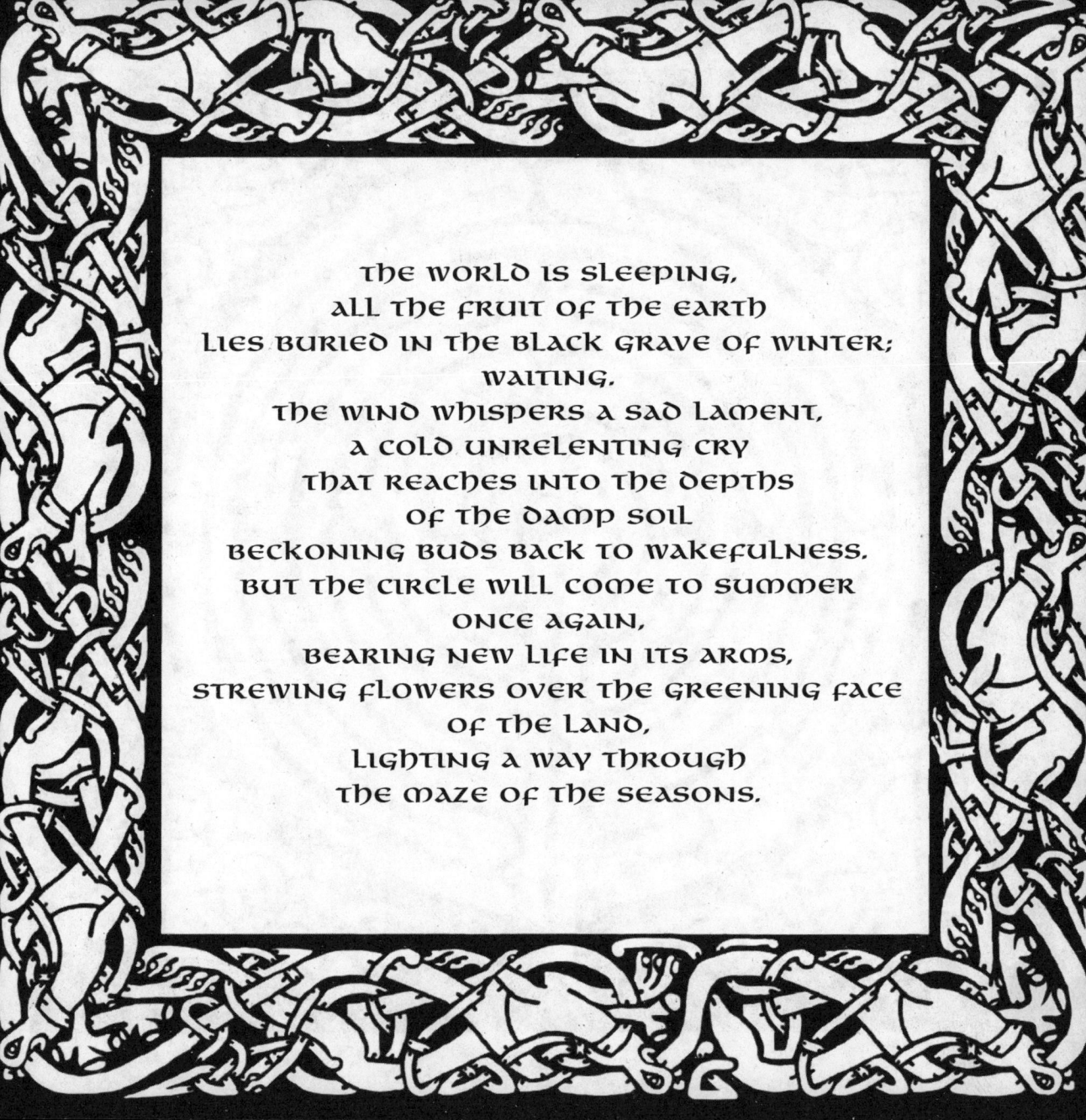

the world is sleeping,
all the fruit of the earth
lies buried in the black grave of winter;
waiting.
the wind whispers a sad lament,
a cold unrelenting cry
that reaches into the depths
of the damp soil
beckoning buds back to wakefulness.
but the circle will come to summer
once again,
bearing new life in its arms,
strewing flowers over the greening face
of the land,
lighting a way through
the maze of the seasons.

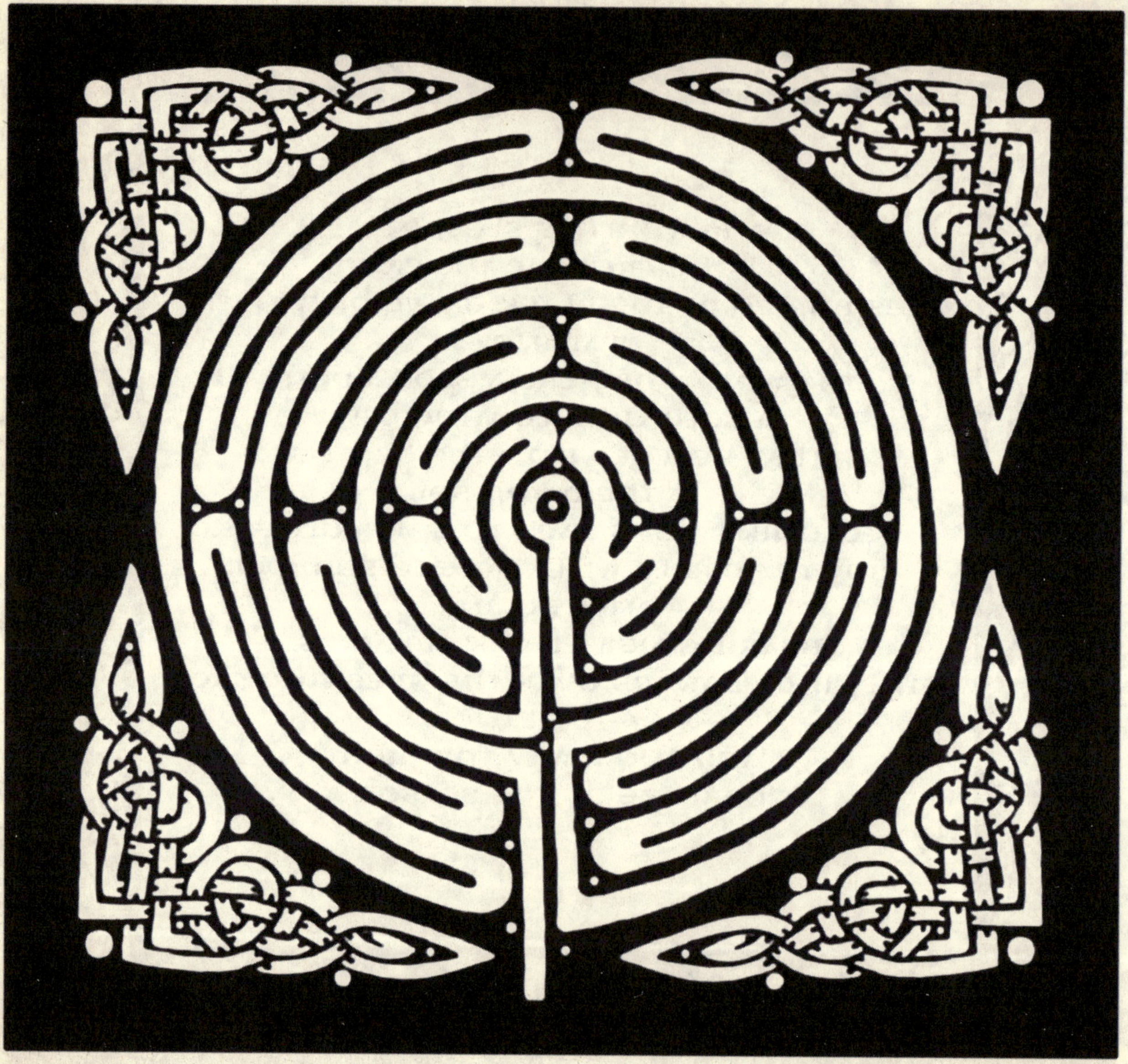

THE FOREST HAS PUT ON
ITS LUSCIOUS COAT OF LIVING GREEN.
THE KING OF SUMMER SITS
AT THE HIGH-TABLE,
LISTENING TO THE SWEET STRUMMING
OF GOLDEN HARP STRINGS.
BUT THE WHITE WINTER WILL RETURN
AND THE HARP WILL HANG UNTOUCHED AGAIN
AMONG THE BARREN BRANCHES
UNTIL THE SUN SAILS HOME.

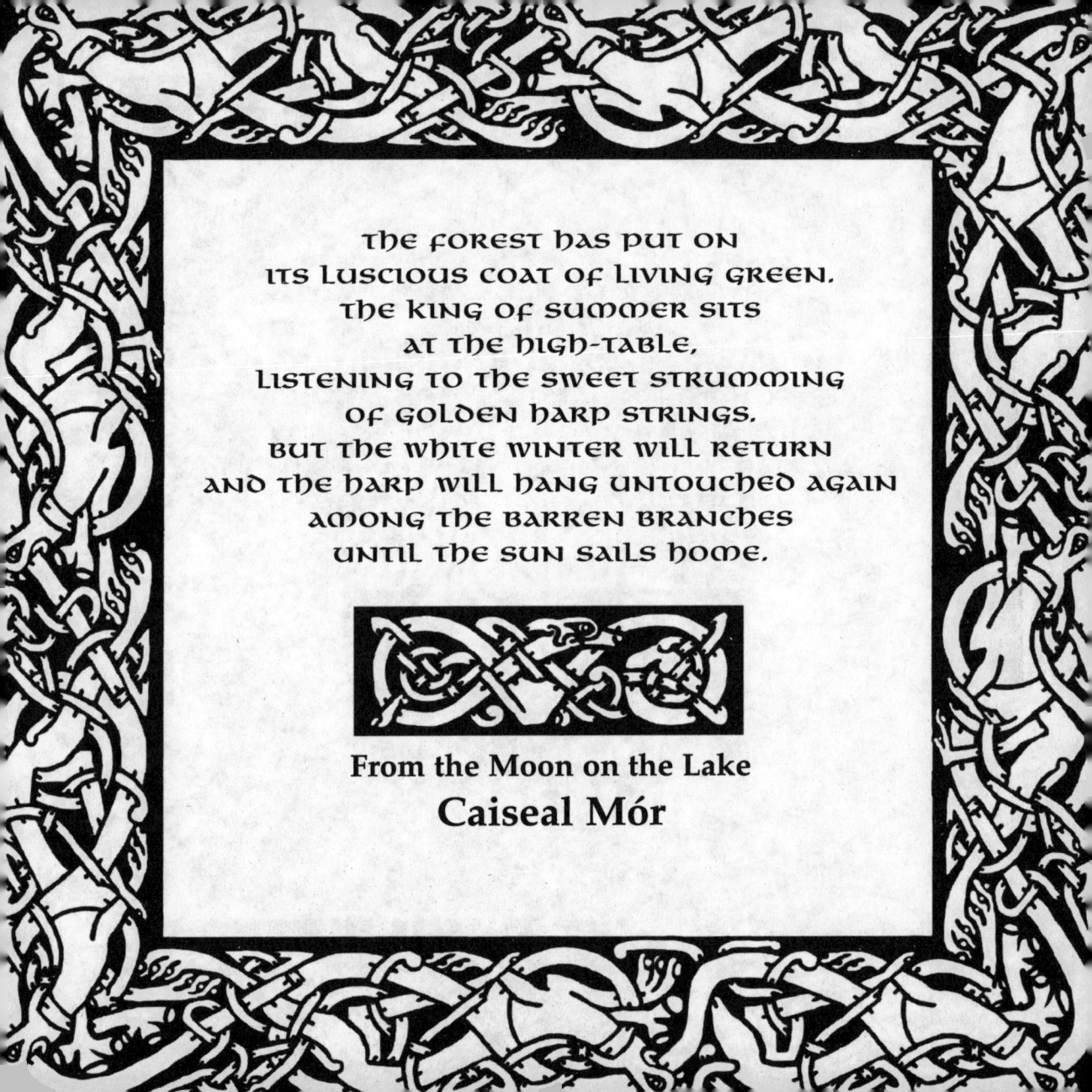

From the Moon on the Lake
Caiseal Mór

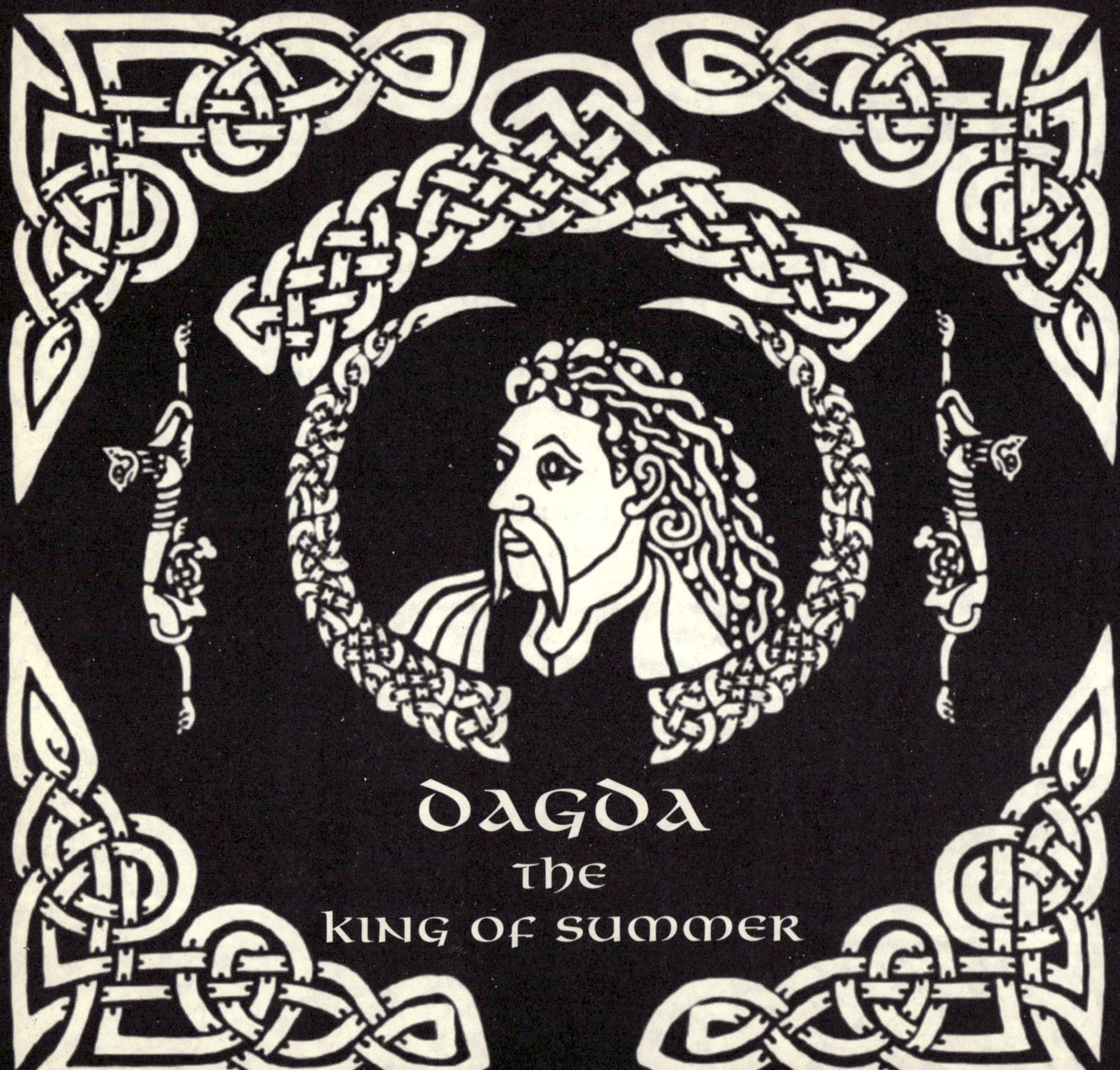
DAGDA
THE
KING OF SUMMER

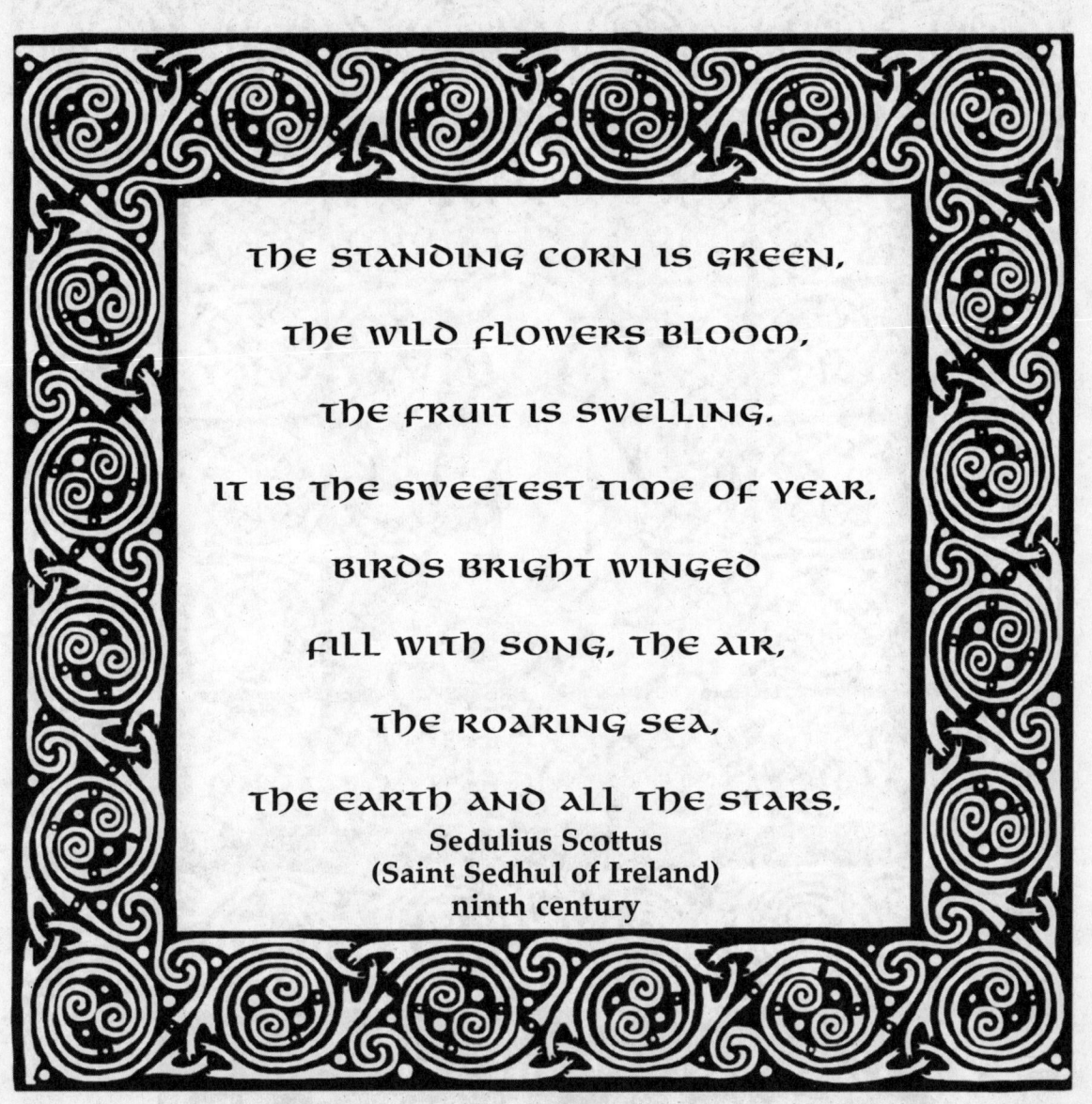

THE STANDING CORN IS GREEN,

THE WILD FLOWERS BLOOM,

THE FRUIT IS SWELLING.

IT IS THE SWEETEST TIME OF YEAR.

BIRDS BRIGHT WINGED

FILL WITH SONG, THE AIR,

THE ROARING SEA,

THE EARTH AND ALL THE STARS.

Sedulius Scottus
(Saint Sedhul of Ireland)
ninth century

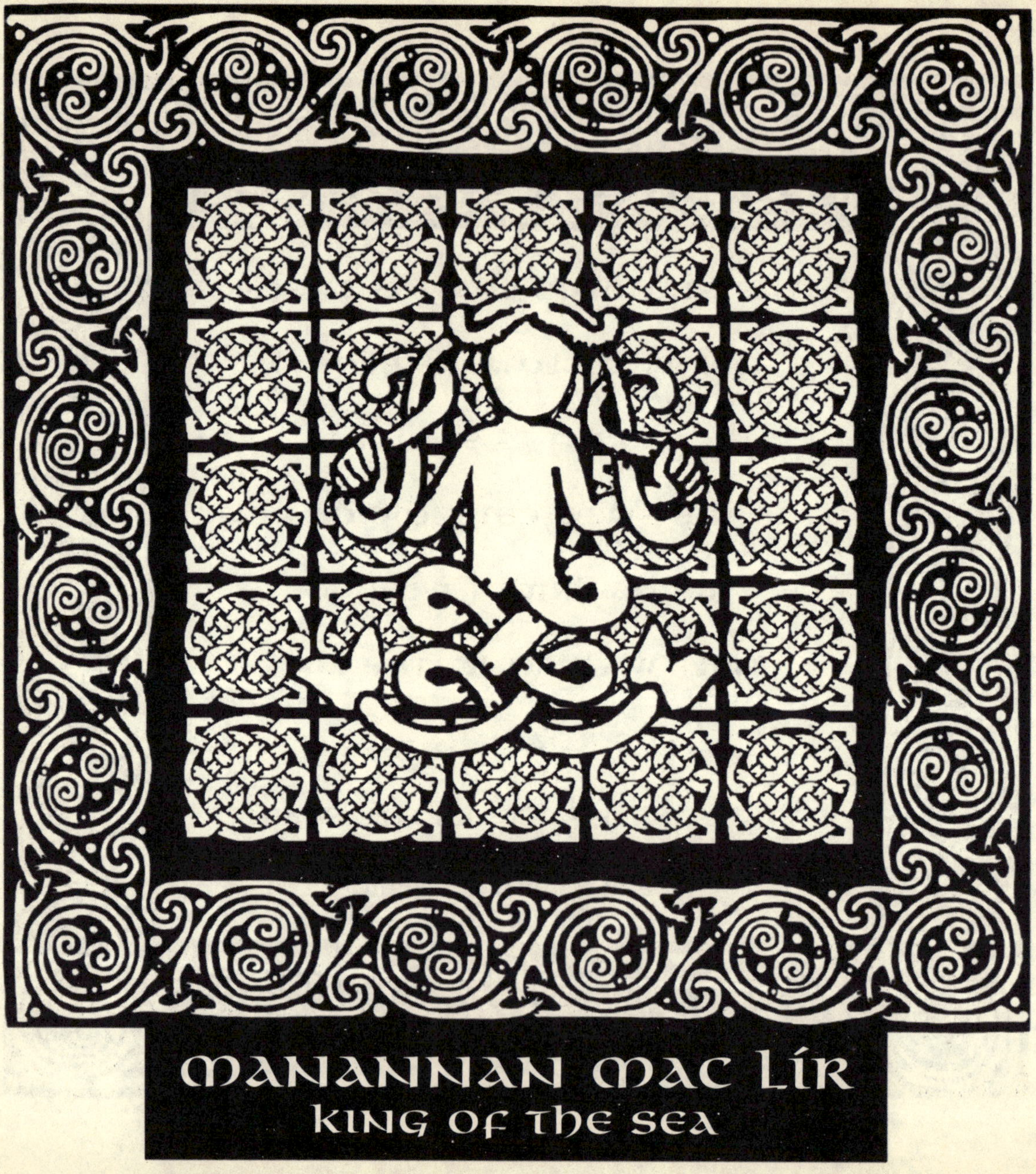

MANANNAN MAC LÍR
KING OF THE SEA

Is achep in ʒáith innocht, fu-fúapna
faipʒʒe find folt, Ní áʒop péimm
mopa minn, Dond láechpaid láinn ó
Lochláinn:·

BITTER IS THE WIND TONIGHT
IT TOSSES THE OCEAN'S WHITE
HAIR.
THIS NIGHT I FEAR NOT THE
COMING FROM OVER THE SEA
OF THE FIERCE WARRIORS OF
THE NORSE.

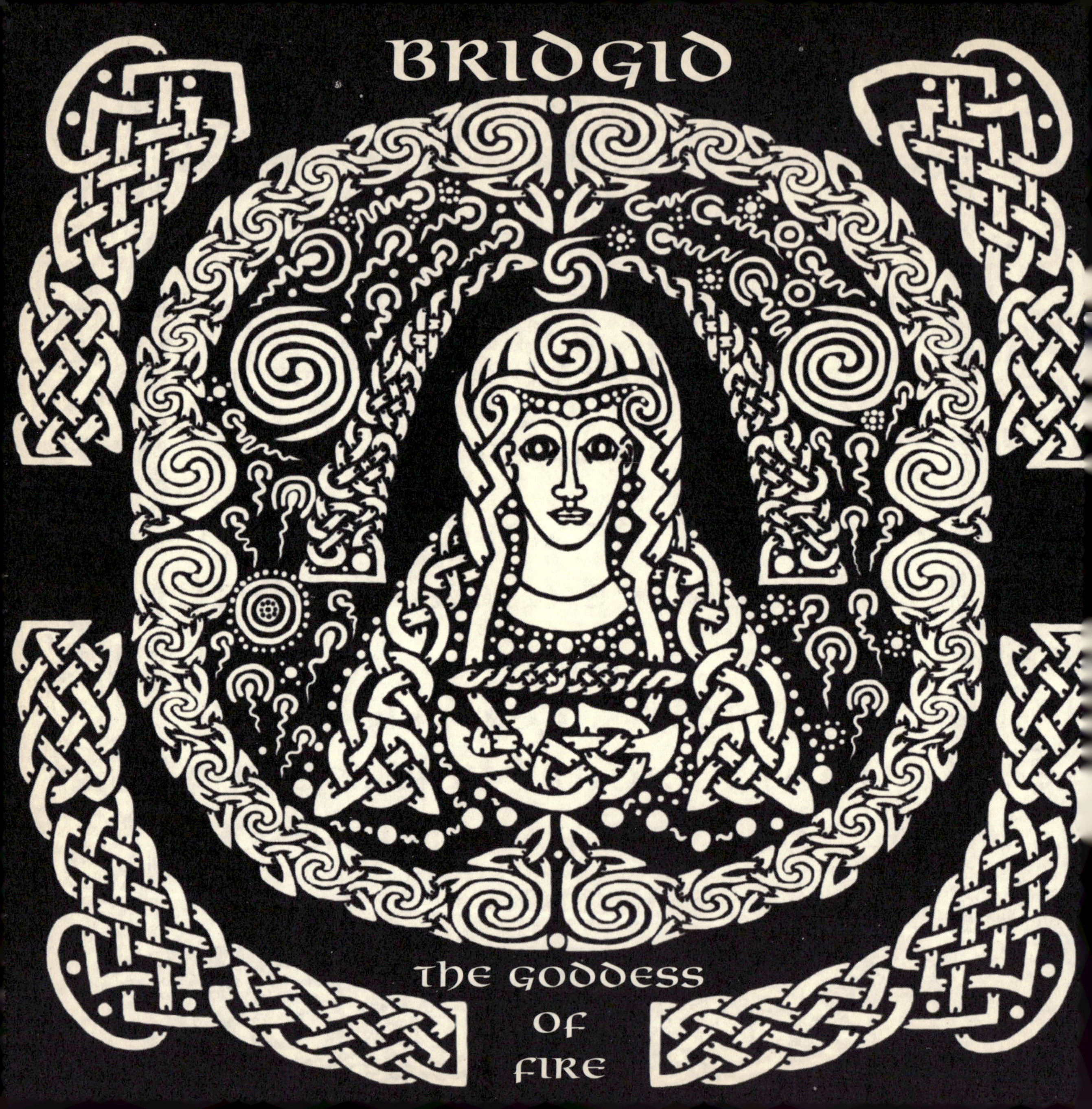
BRIDGID
THE GODDESS
OF
FIRE

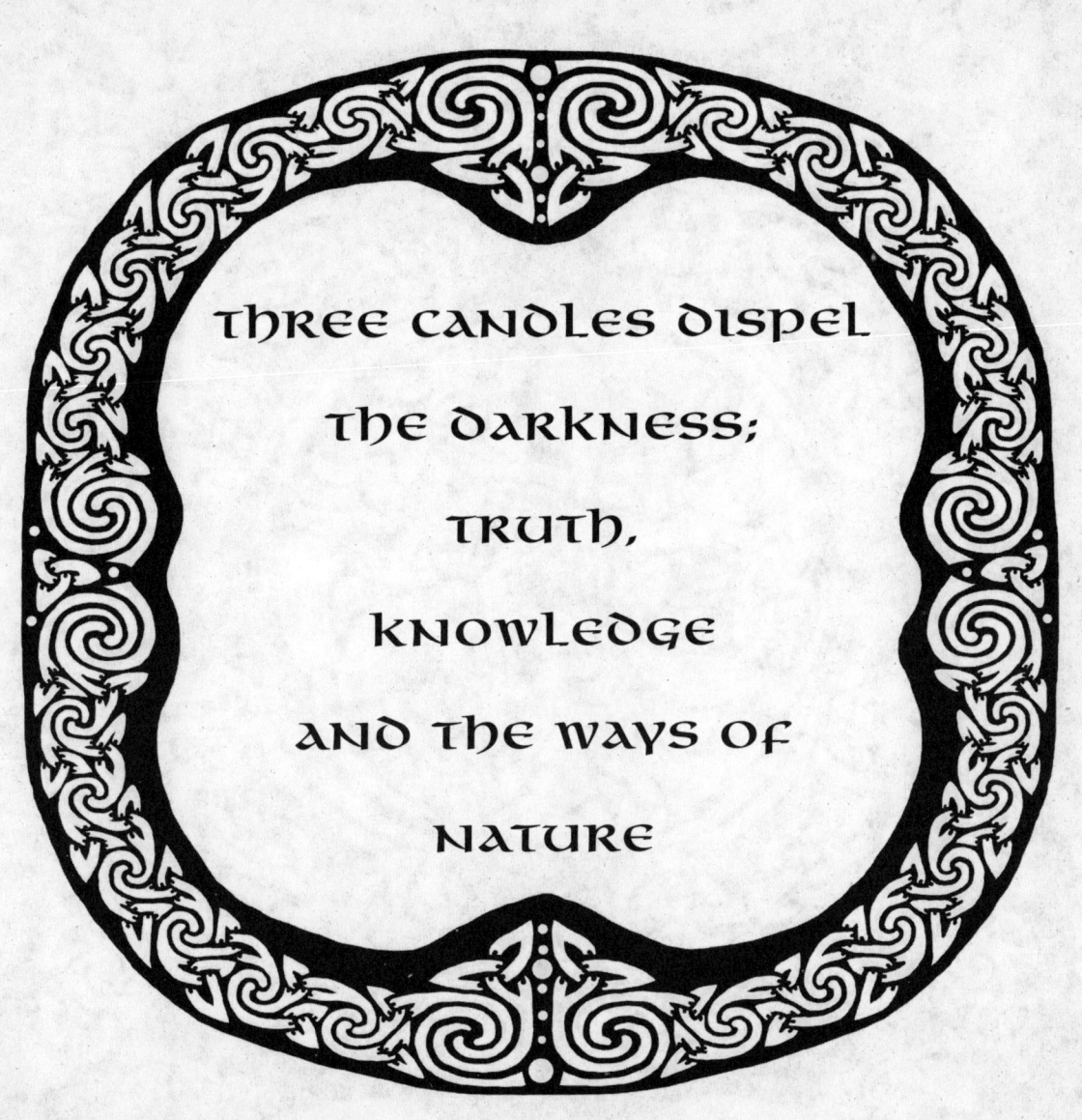

THREE CANDLES DISPEL

THE DARKNESS;

TRUTH,

KNOWLEDGE

AND THE WAYS OF

NATURE

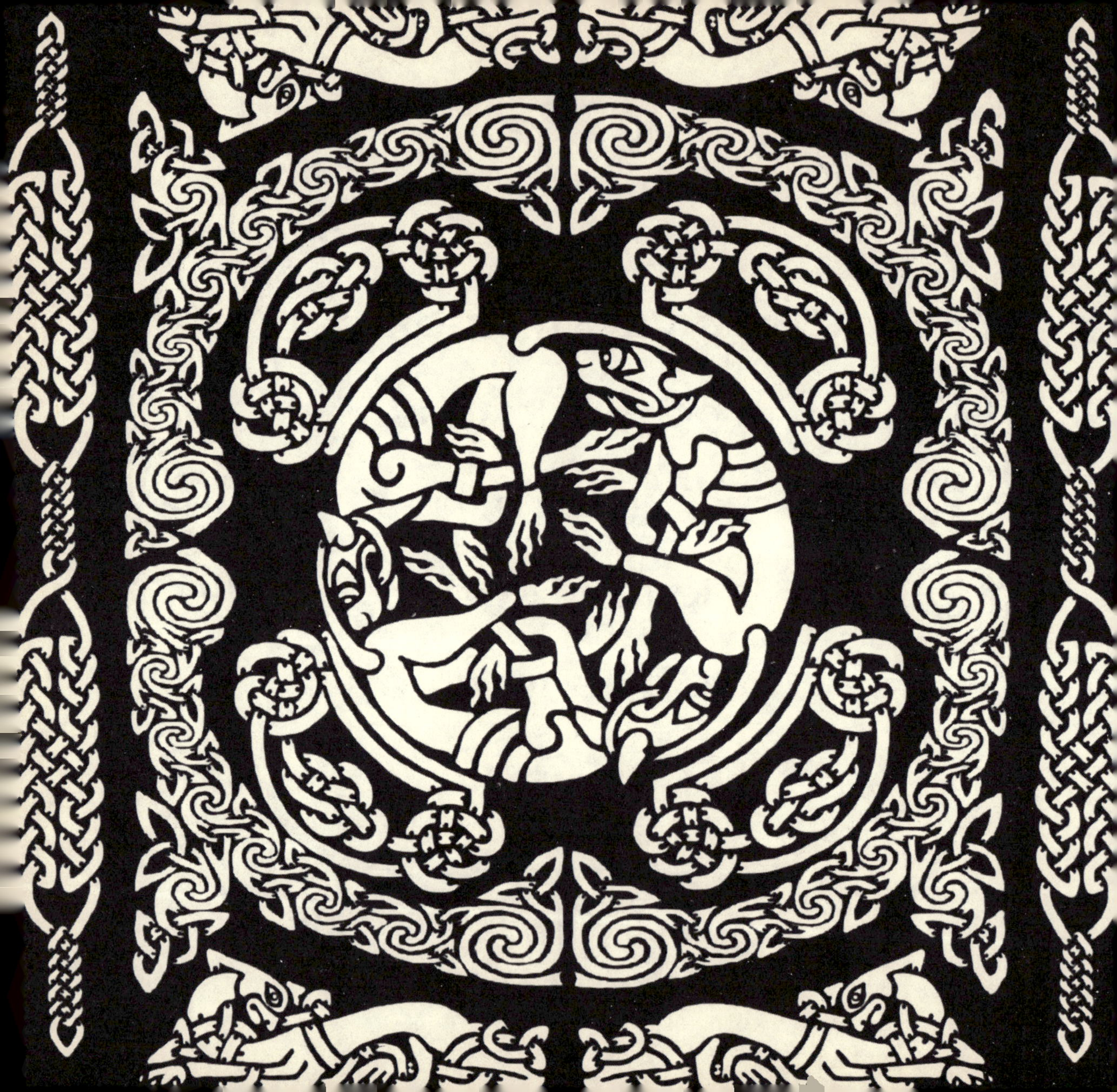

DRESS A GOAT

IN SILK

AND IT'S STILL

A GOAT

AMAIRGEN'S DREAM

I AM THE WIND ON THE SEA,

I AM THE WAVE ON THE OCEAN,

I AM THE ROAR OF THE SEA,

I AM A STAG OF SEVEN POINTS,

I AM A BULL OF SEVEN FIGHTS,

I AM A HAWK ON A CLIFF,

I AM A TEAR-DROP OF THE SUN,

I AM THE FAIREST OF BLOSSOMS,

I AM A BOAR OF BOLDNESS,

I AM A SALMON IN A POOL,

I AM A LAKE ON A PLAIN,

I AM THE STOREHOUSE OF POETRY,

I AM A WORD OF SKILL,

I AM A CORNER IN A MAZE,

I AM THE TOMB OF EVERY HOPE.

WHO BUT I MENDS THE TORN THATCH OF WOUNDS?

WHO BUT I KNOWS THE SECRETS OF THE STONE DOOR?

WHO HAS SEVEN TIMES SOUGHT THE PLACES OF PEACE?

WHO, SAVE I, KNOWS THE AGES OF THE MOON,

THE PLACE AND TIME THE SUN SETS?

WHO CALLS THE CATTLE FROM TETHRA'S HOUSE,

AND SEES THEM DANCE IN THE BRIGHT HEAVENS?

WHO SHAPES THE WEAPONS IN A STRONGHOLD OF GLASS?

WHO BUT THE POET, THE SINGER OF PRAISE-SONGS,

WHO BUT I READS THE SECRET LETTERS OF THE OGHAM,

SCRAPED ON STONES?

WHO KEEPS THE TWO ARMIES SEPARATE?

I, WHO AM THE WIND ON THE SEA.

When the Gaels first landed in Ireland their Chief Poet, Amairgen,
had a strange dream which foretold that he would spend many lifetimes
in this new land. The Gaels took the poem that came from his dream
to mean that they had successfully conquered the island.

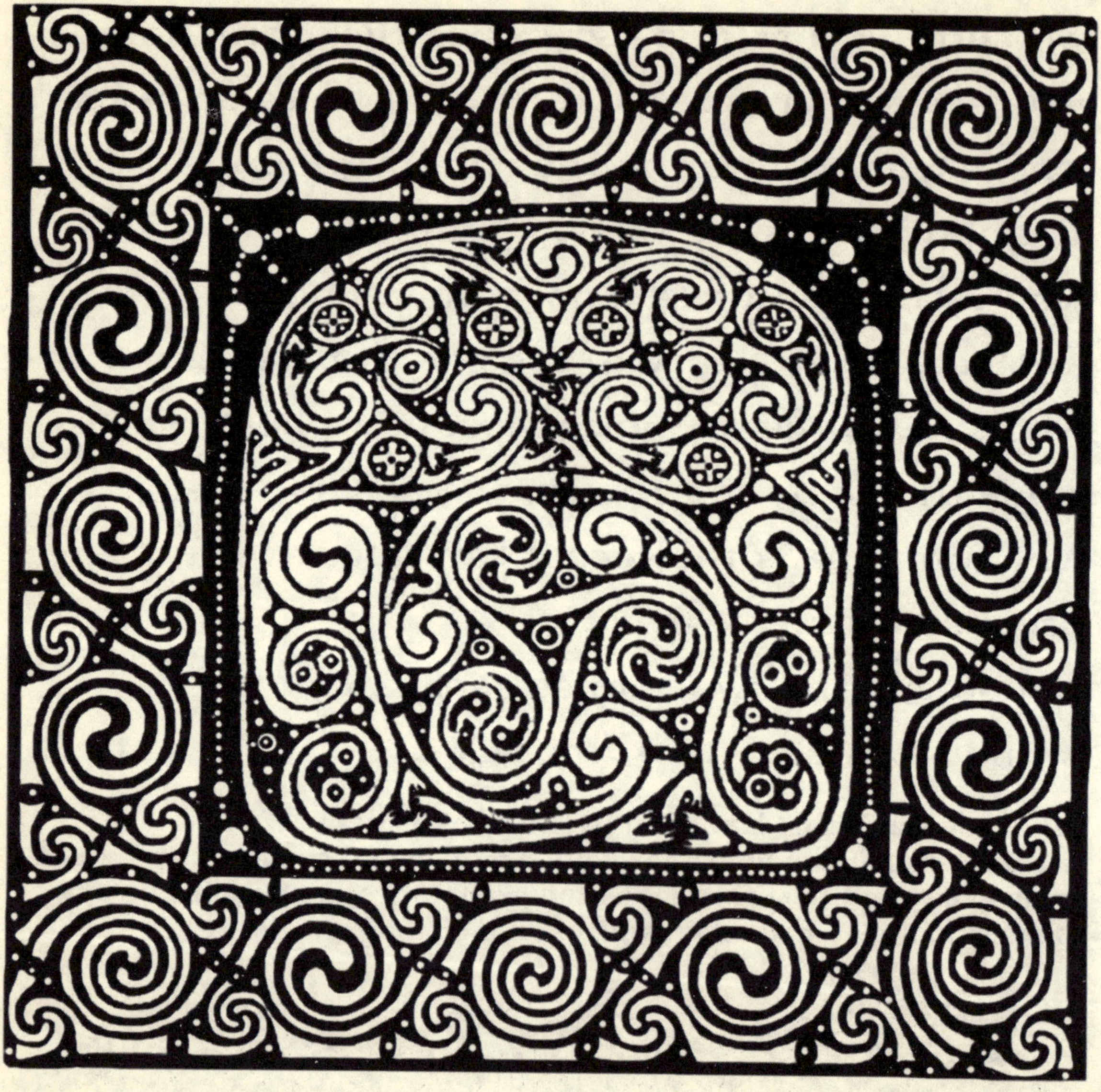

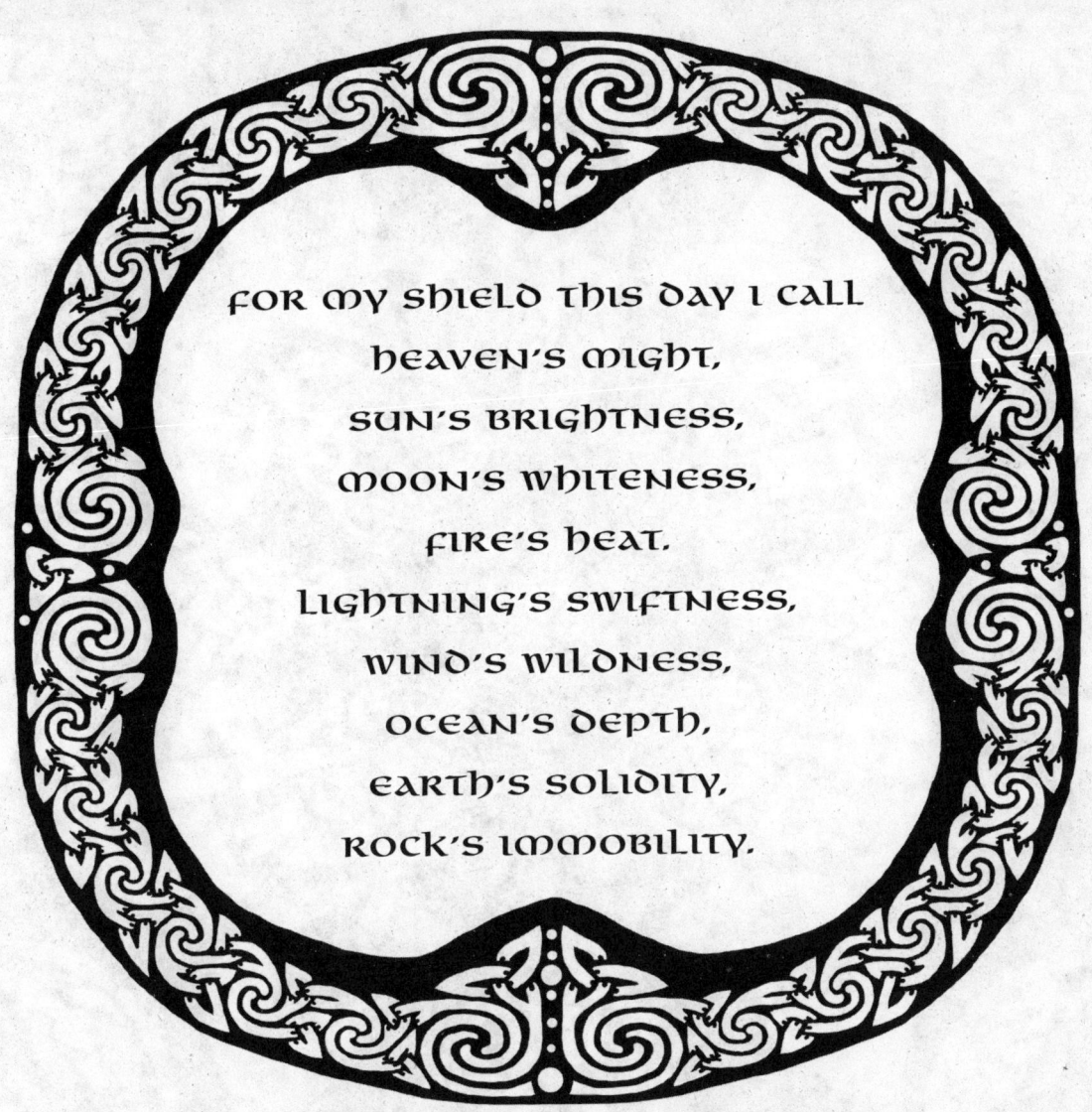

FOR MY SHIELD THIS DAY I CALL
HEAVEN'S MIGHT,
SUN'S BRIGHTNESS,
MOON'S WHITENESS,
FIRE'S HEAT.
LIGHTNING'S SWIFTNESS,
WIND'S WILDNESS,
OCEAN'S DEPTH,
EARTH'S SOLIDITY,
ROCK'S IMMOBILITY.

From the ancient prayer called
the 'Breastplate of Saint Patrick',
attributed to the patron saint of Ireland.

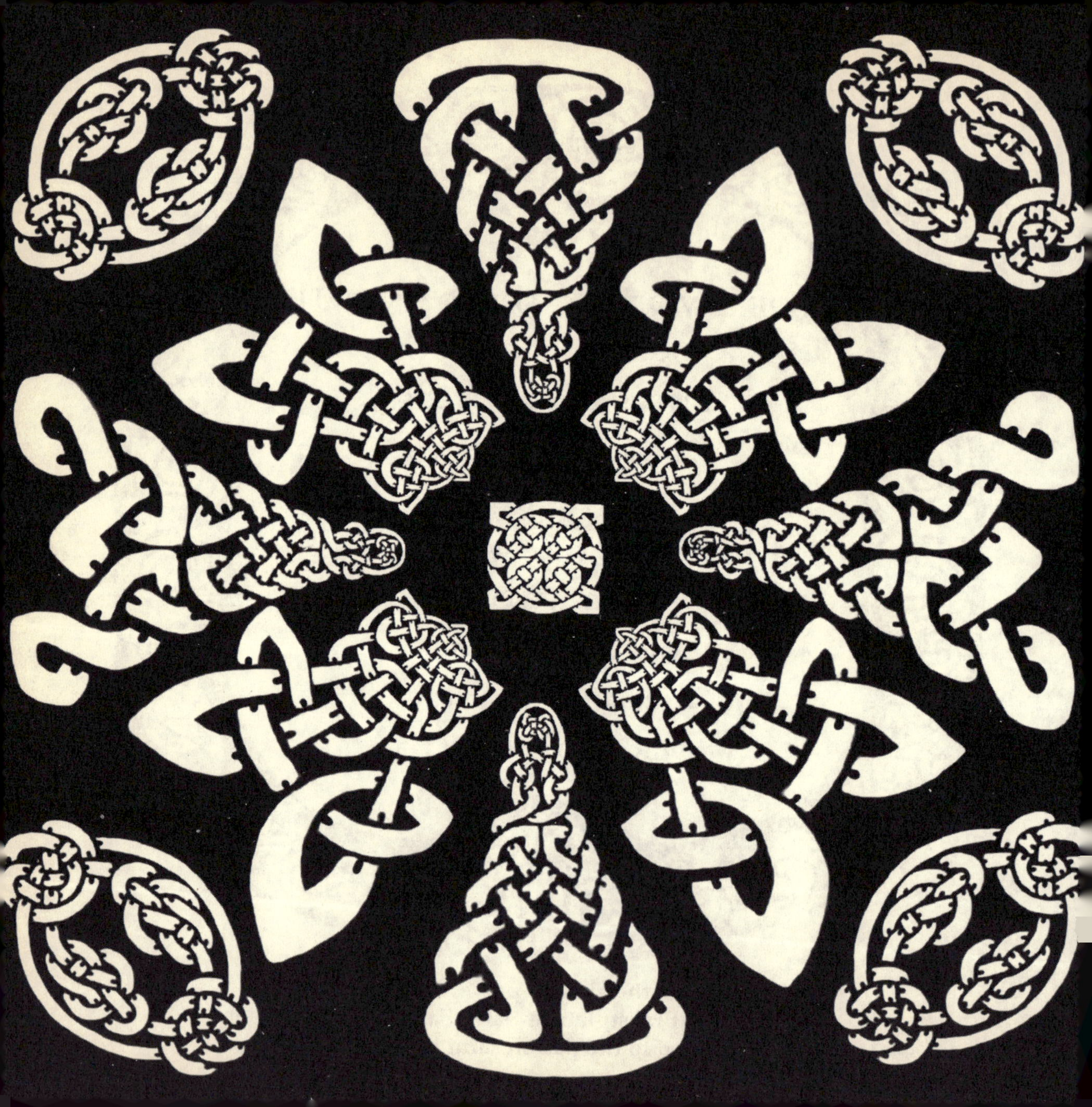

GREETING TO YOU,

GEM OF THE NIGHT,

BEAUTY OF THE SKIES,

GEM OF THE NIGHT,

MOTHER OF THE STARS,

GEM OF THE NIGHT,

FOSTER-CHILD OF THE SUN,

GEM OF THE NIGHT,

MAJESTY OF THE HEAVENS,

GEM OF THE NIGHT.

Carmina Gadelica

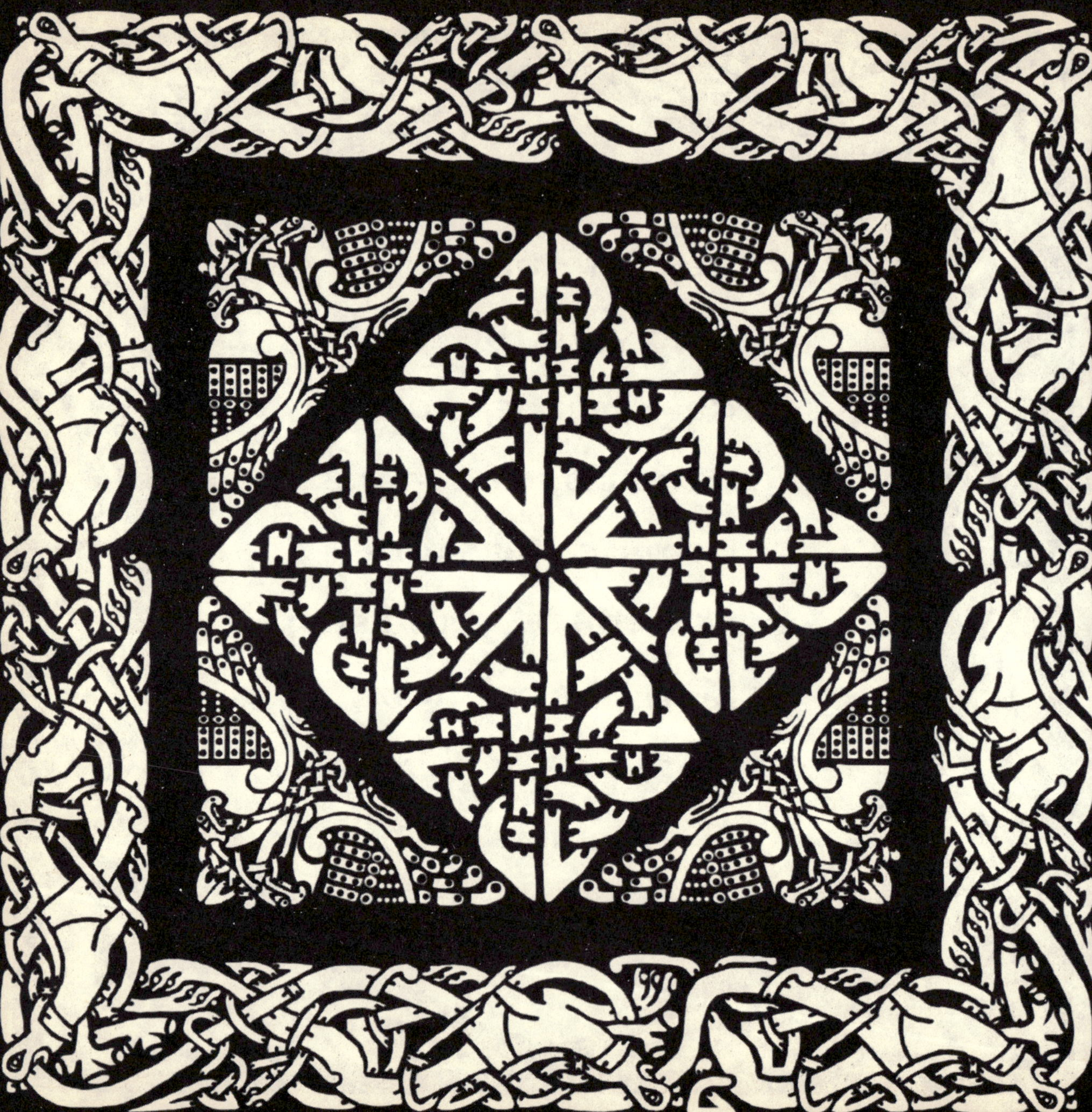

YOU ARE WHITER THAN A SWAN ON THE LAKE.

YOU ARE WHITER THAN THE SEAGULL ON THE GREEN OCEAN.

YOU ARE WHITER THAN THE SNOW OF THE HIGH MOUNTAINS.

YOU ARE THE LOVELY RED ROWAN

THAT CALMS THE ANGER OF MEN.

LIKE A WAVE OF THE SEA FROM FLOOD TO EBB.

LIKE A WAVE OF THE SEA FROM EBB TO FLOOD.

Carmina Gadelica

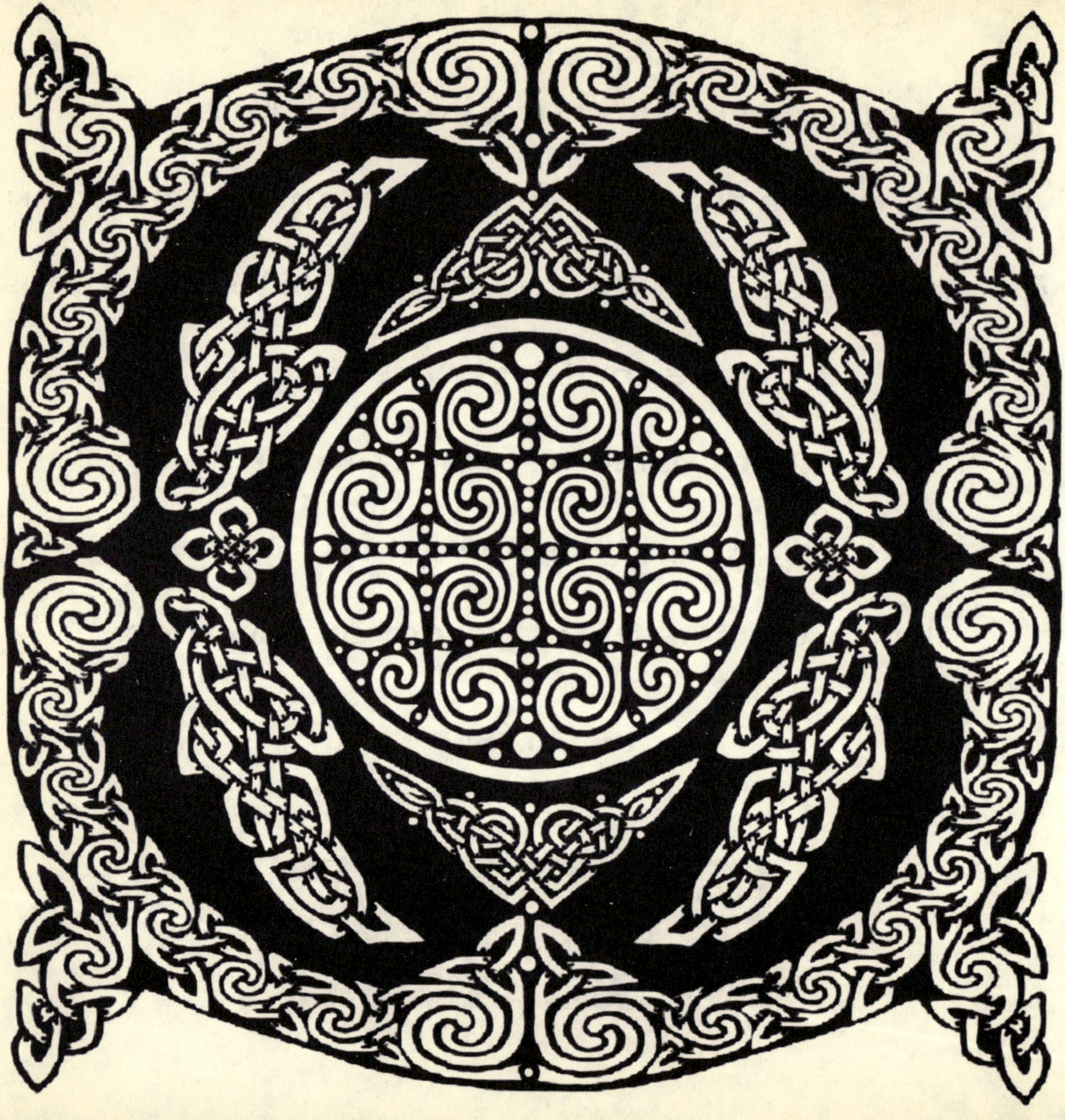

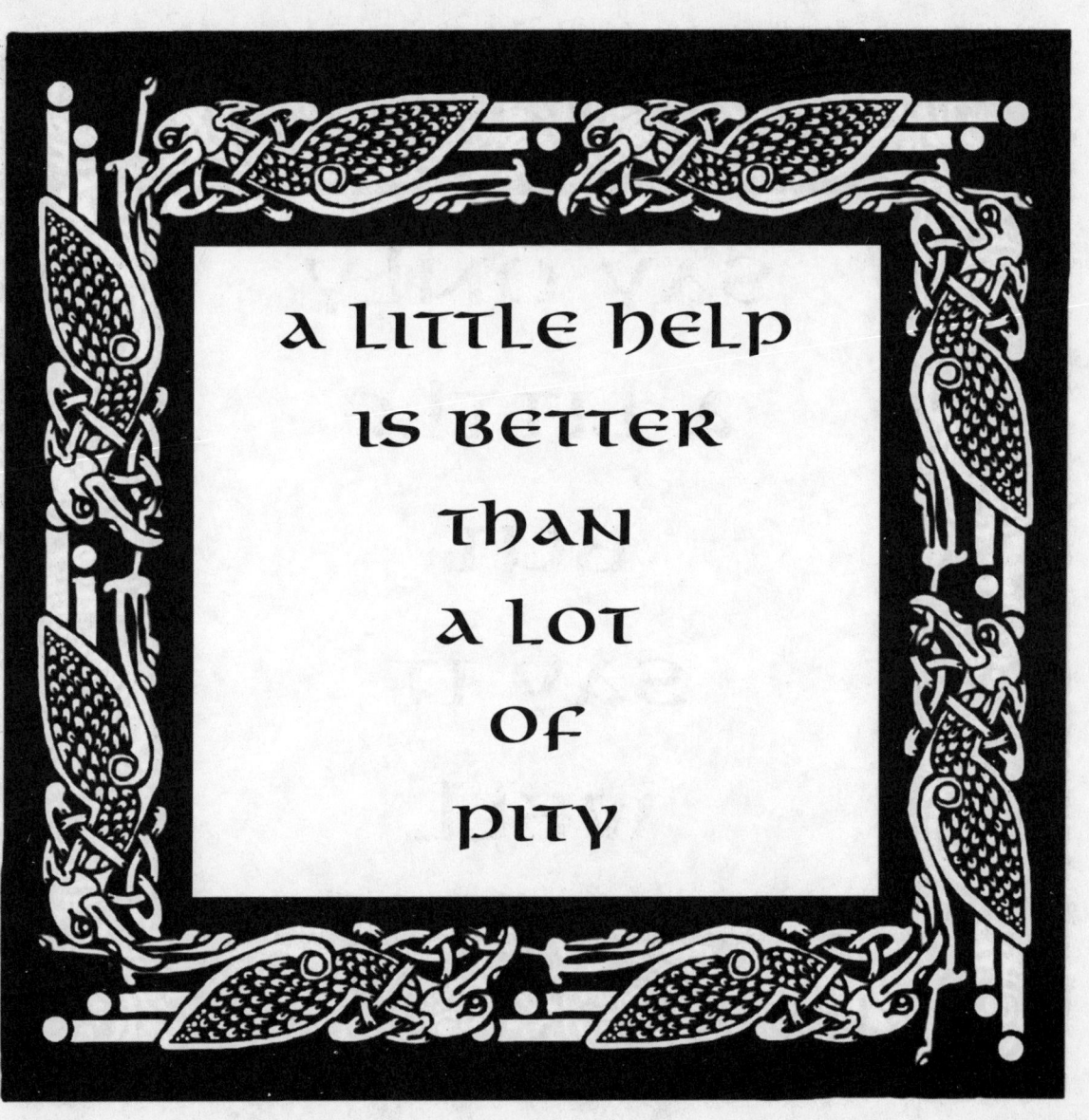

A LITTLE HELP
IS BETTER
THAN
A LOT
OF
PITY

say only
a little
but
say it
well

THE NOBLEST SHARE OF EARTH IS IN THE FAR WEST OF THE WORLD,

WHOSE NAME IS WRITTEN EIRINN IN THE BOOKS OF OLD.

RICH IN GOODS, IN SILVER, JEWELS, CLOTH AND GOLD.

A FAIR PLACE WITH CLEAR AIR AND MELLOW SOIL.

POISON HARMS NO-ONE THERE.

NO SERPENT GLIDES IN THE GRASS.

NO LOUD FROGS SING HARSHLY IN THE LAKES.

WORTHY ARE THE PEOPLE WHO LIVE IN THAT COUNTRY.

THEY ARE A RACE RENOWNED IN WAR AND PEACE.

AND RENOWNED FOR THEIR FAITH.

Donatus, and Irish missionary who rose to become Bishop of Fiesole
in Italy. He never returned home.

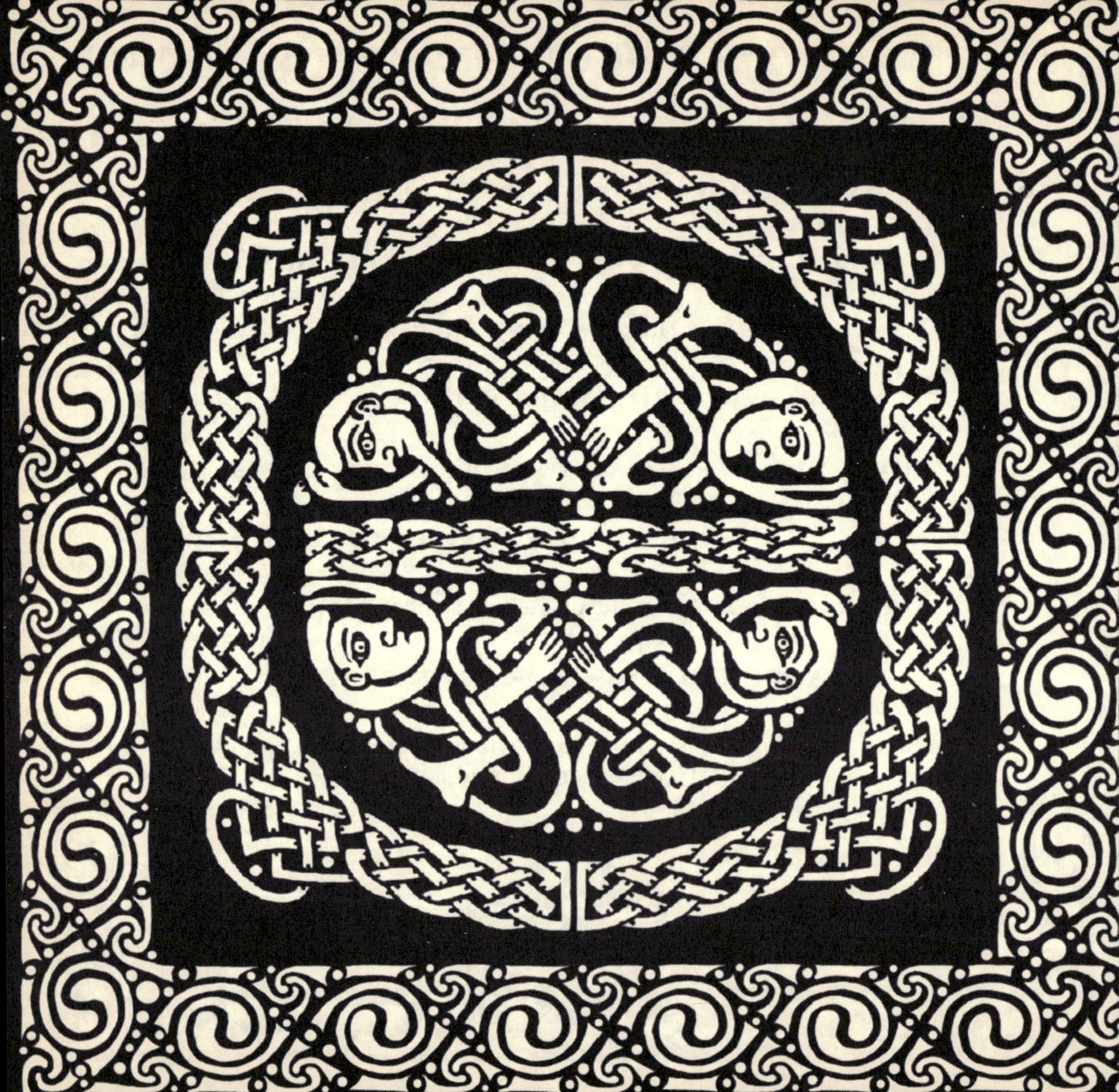

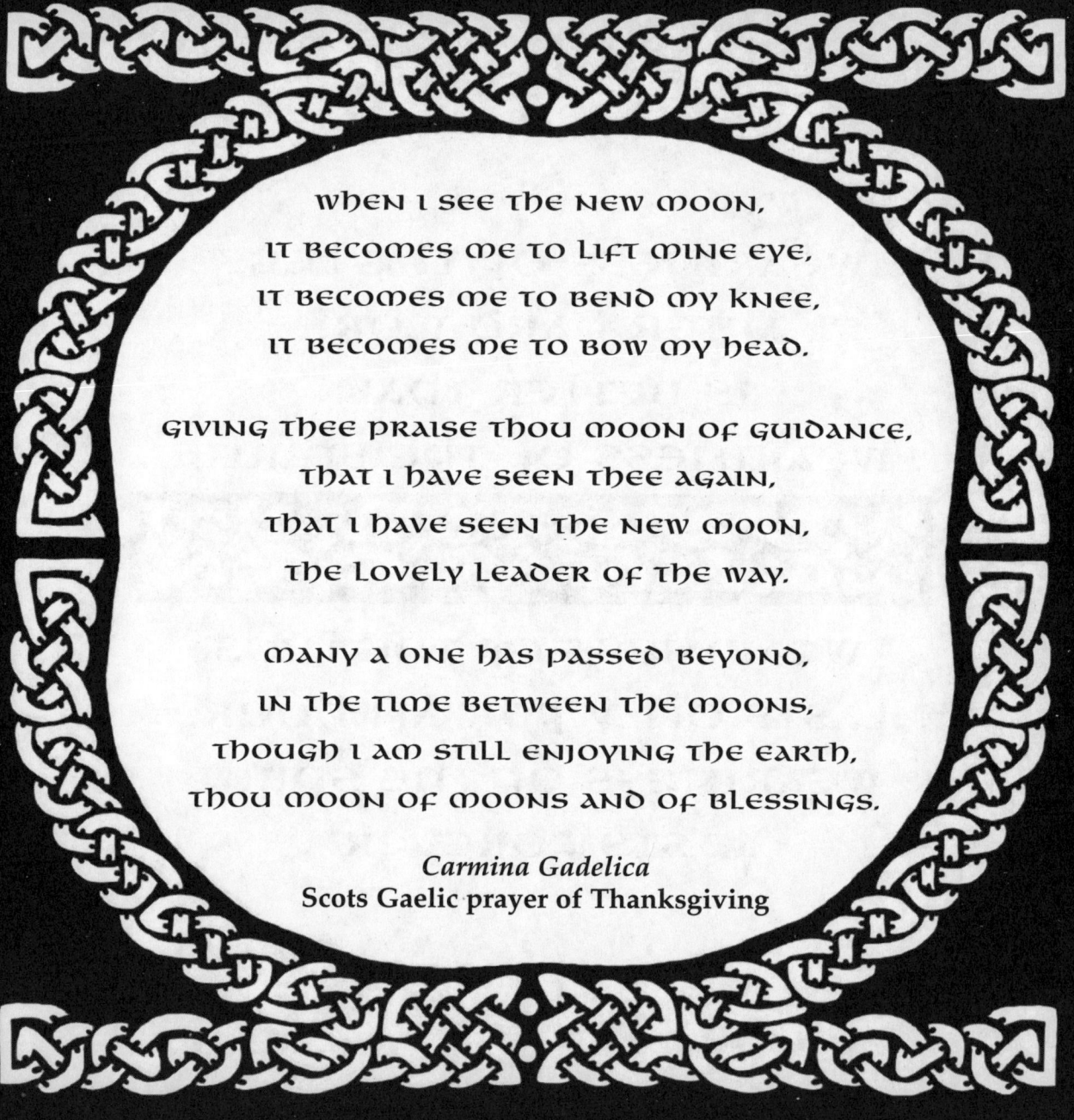

WHEN I SEE THE NEW MOON,
IT BECOMES ME TO LIFT MINE EYE,
IT BECOMES ME TO BEND MY KNEE,
IT BECOMES ME TO BOW MY HEAD.

GIVING THEE PRAISE THOU MOON OF GUIDANCE,
THAT I HAVE SEEN THEE AGAIN,
THAT I HAVE SEEN THE NEW MOON,
THE LOVELY LEADER OF THE WAY.

MANY A ONE HAS PASSED BEYOND,
IN THE TIME BETWEEN THE MOONS,
THOUGH I AM STILL ENJOYING THE EARTH,
THOU MOON OF MOONS AND OF BLESSINGS.

Carmina Gadelica
Scots Gaelic prayer of Thanksgiving

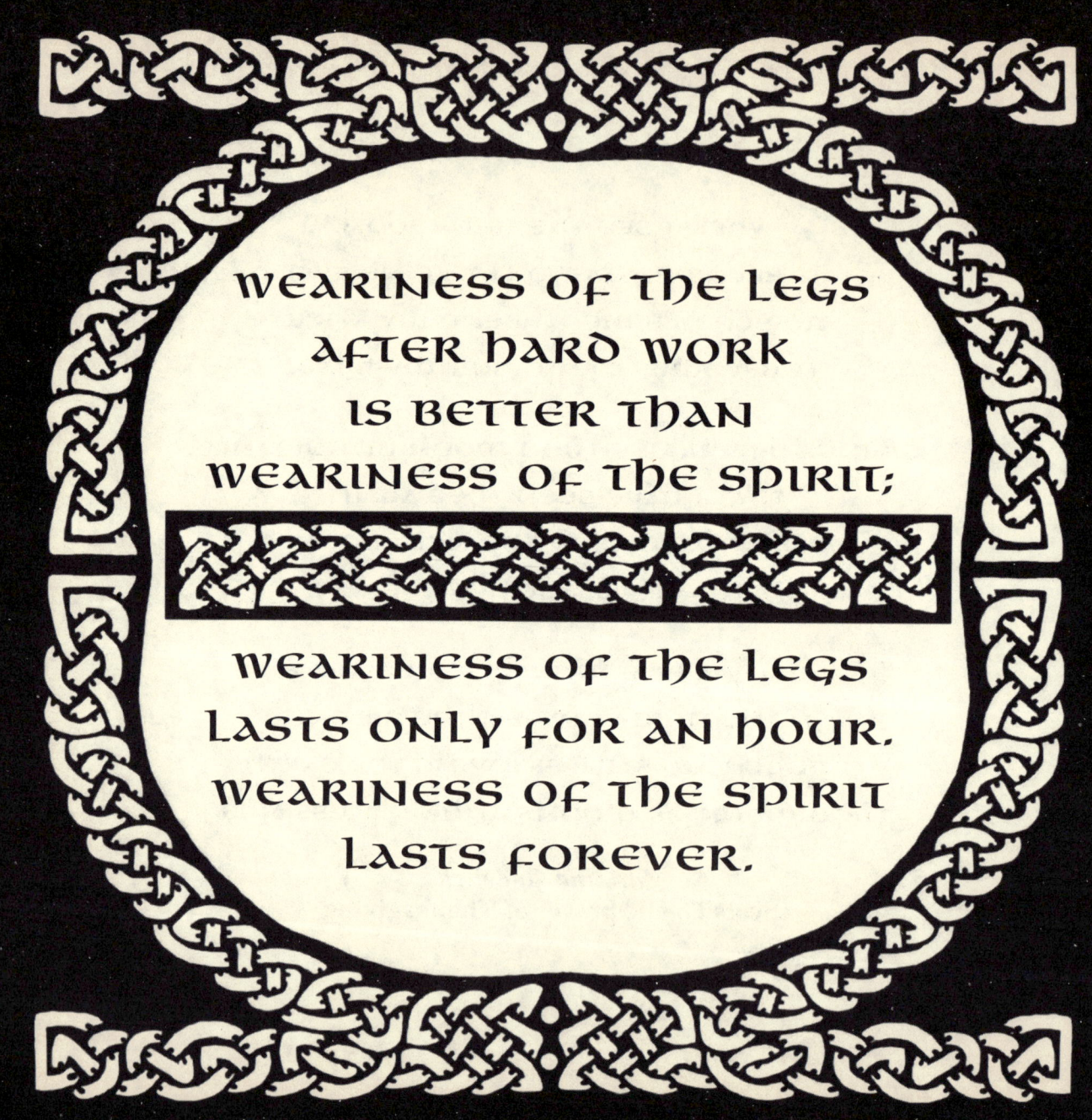

WEARINESS OF THE LEGS
AFTER HARD WORK
IS BETTER THAN
WEARINESS OF THE SPIRIT;

WEARINESS OF THE LEGS
LASTS ONLY FOR AN HOUR.
WEARINESS OF THE SPIRIT
LASTS FOREVER.

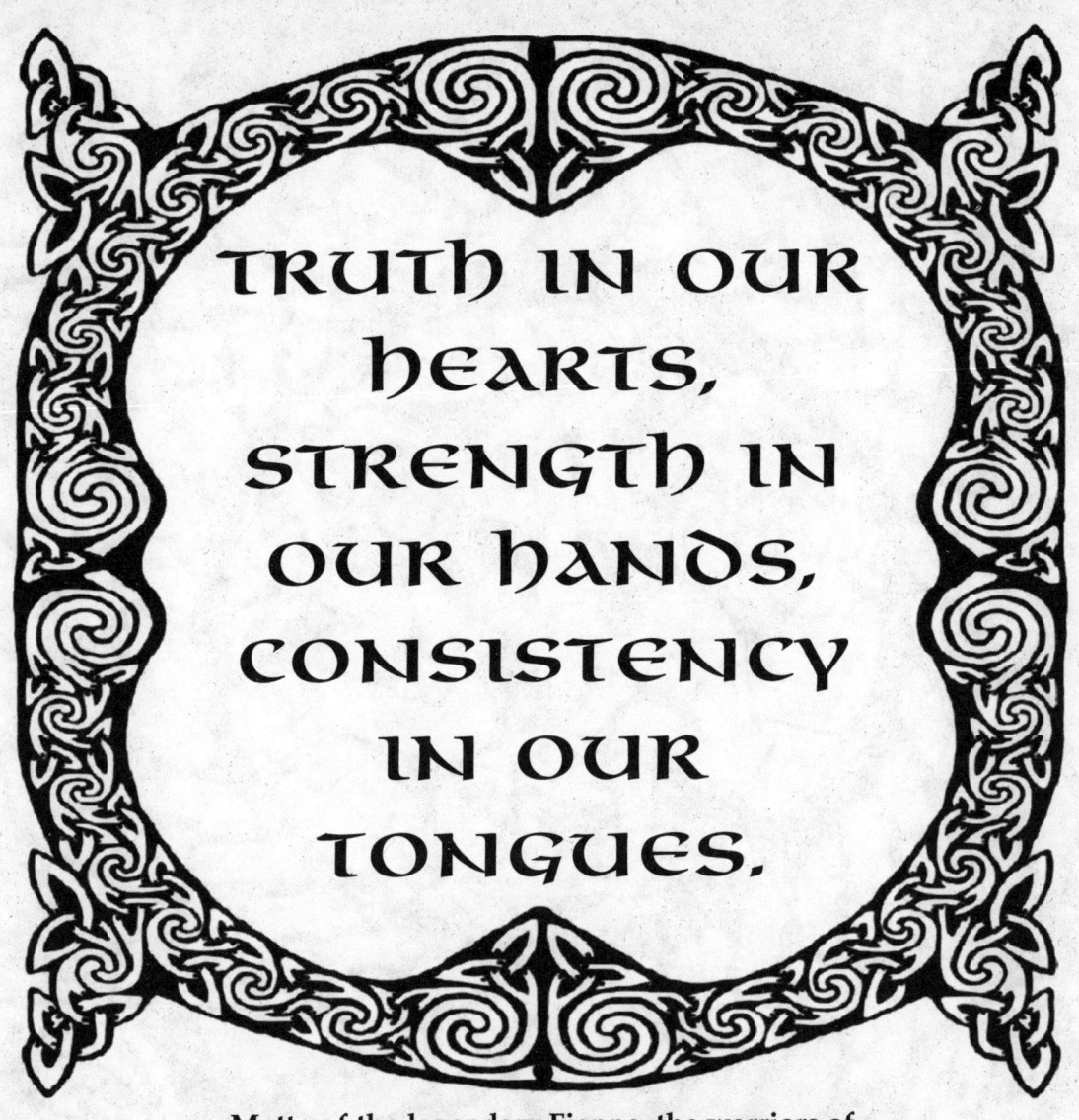

TRUTH IN OUR HEARTS, STRENGTH IN OUR HANDS, CONSISTENCY IN OUR TONGUES.

Motto of the legendary Fianna, the warriors of
Fionn MacCumhal. Being a warrior meant more
than carrying a sword to the ancient Irish.
The concept of honour was very important.

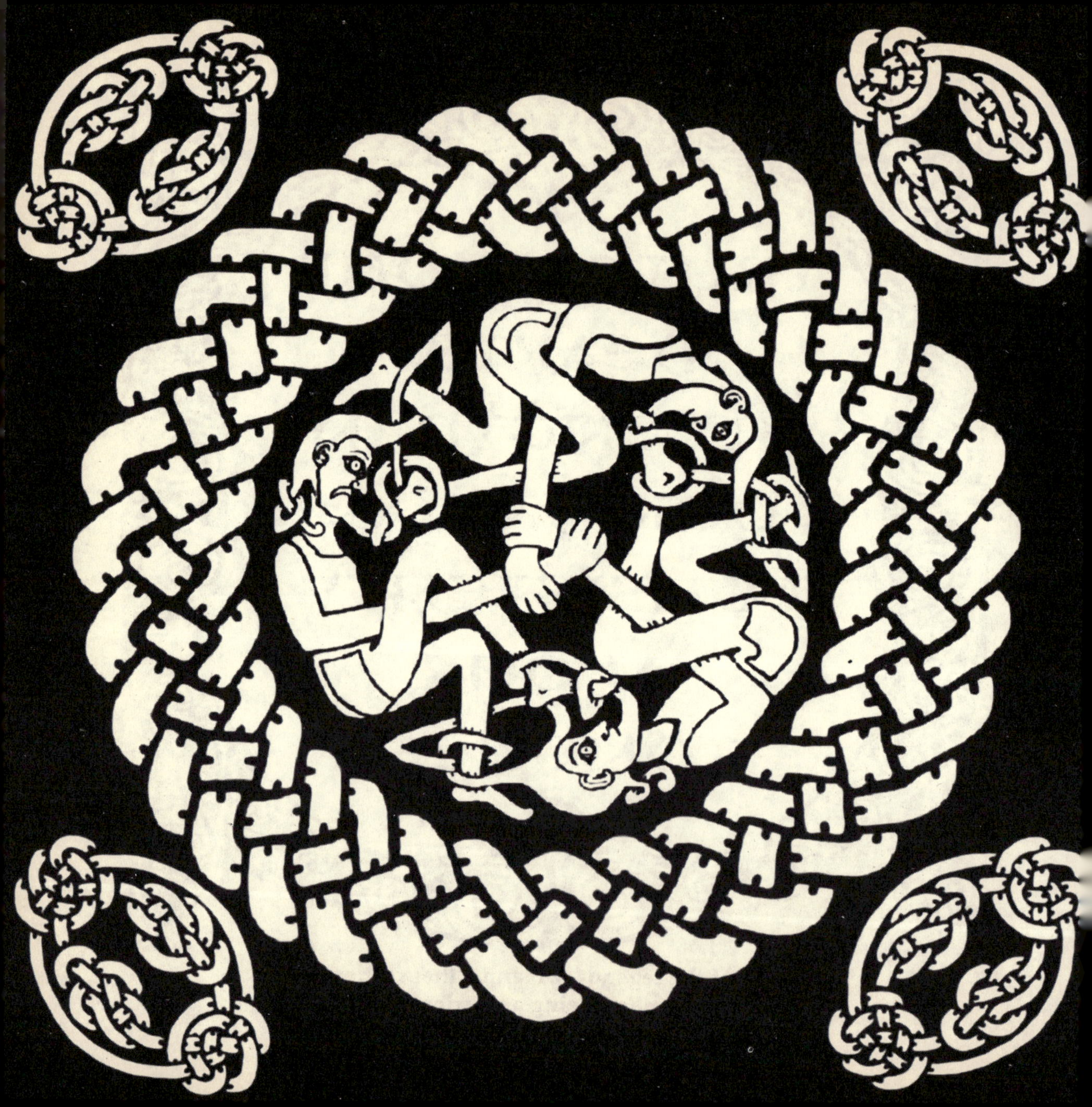

THE SACRED THREE:
TO SAVE,
TO SHIELD,
TO SURROUND,
THE HEARTH,
THE HOUSE,
THE HOUSEHOLD,
THIS EVE,
THIS NIGHT,
ON THIS EVE,
THIS NIGHT,
AND EVERY NIGHT,
EACH SINGLE NIGHT,
AMEN.

Carmina Gadelica

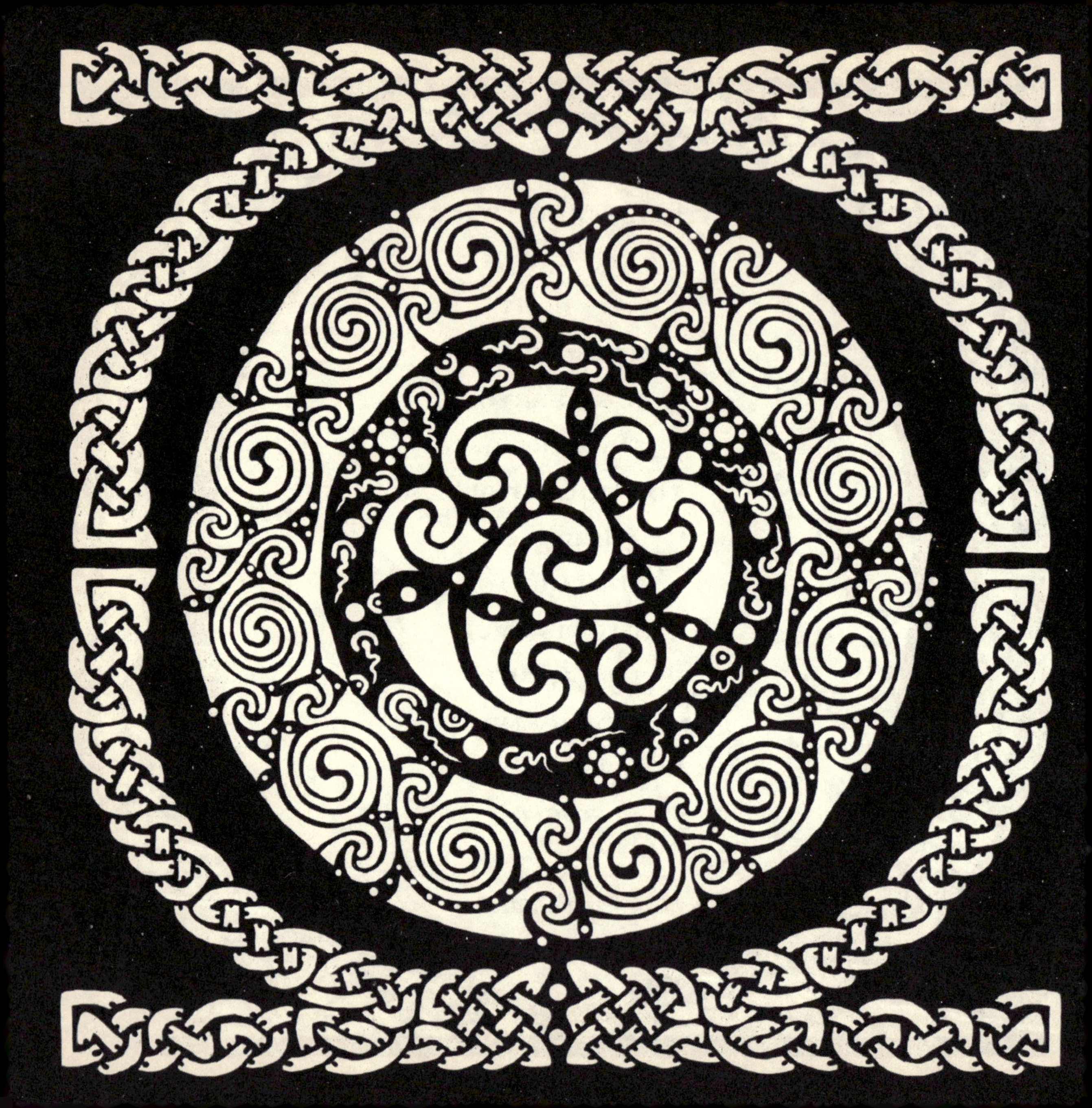

FEEDING THE LAND BEFORE

IT IS STARVING

LETTING IT REST BEFORE

IT IS TIRED OUT

CUTTING BACK THE WEEDS

BEFORE THEY STRANGLE IT

THESE ARE THE MARKS OF

A GOOD FARMER

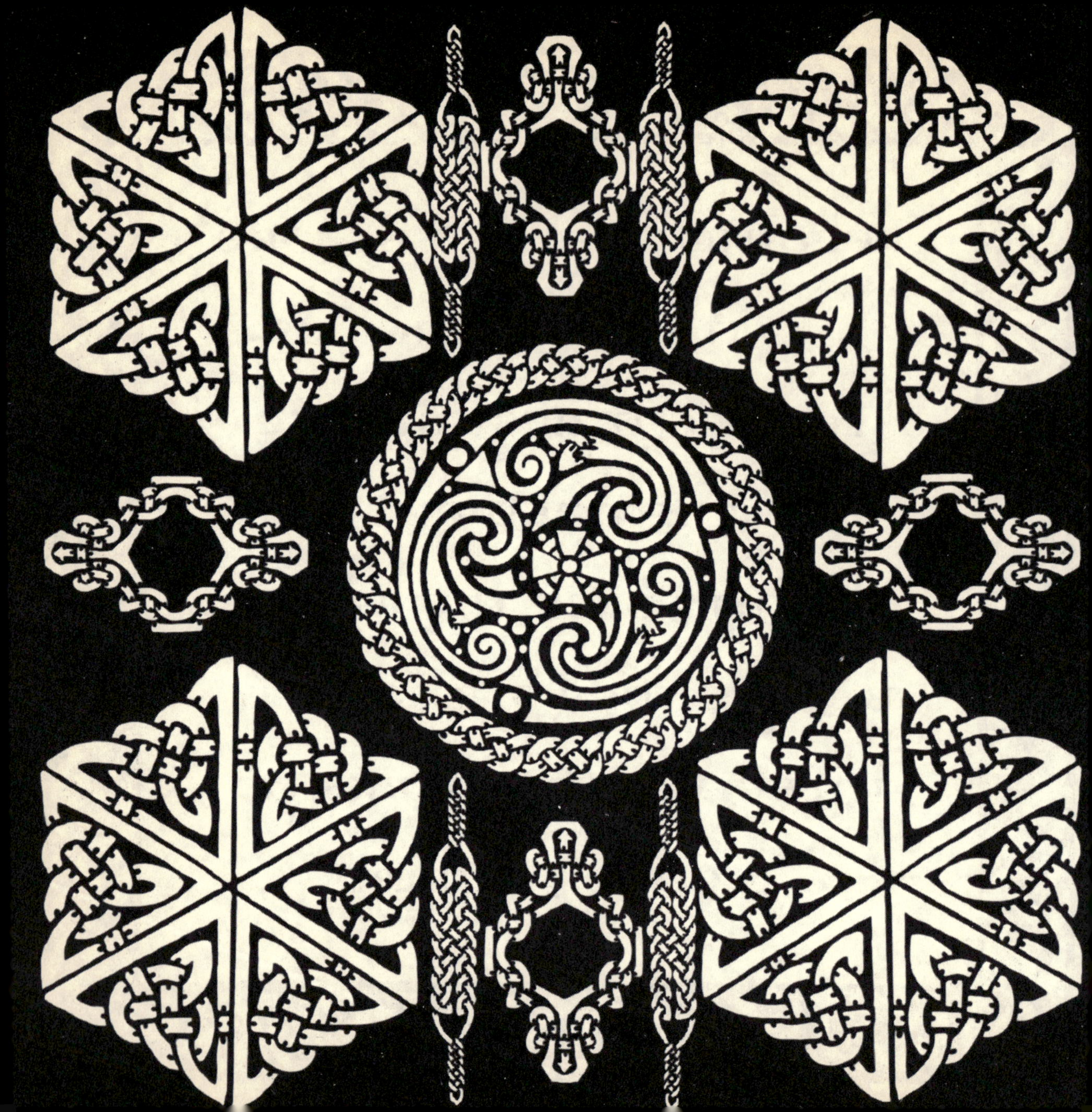

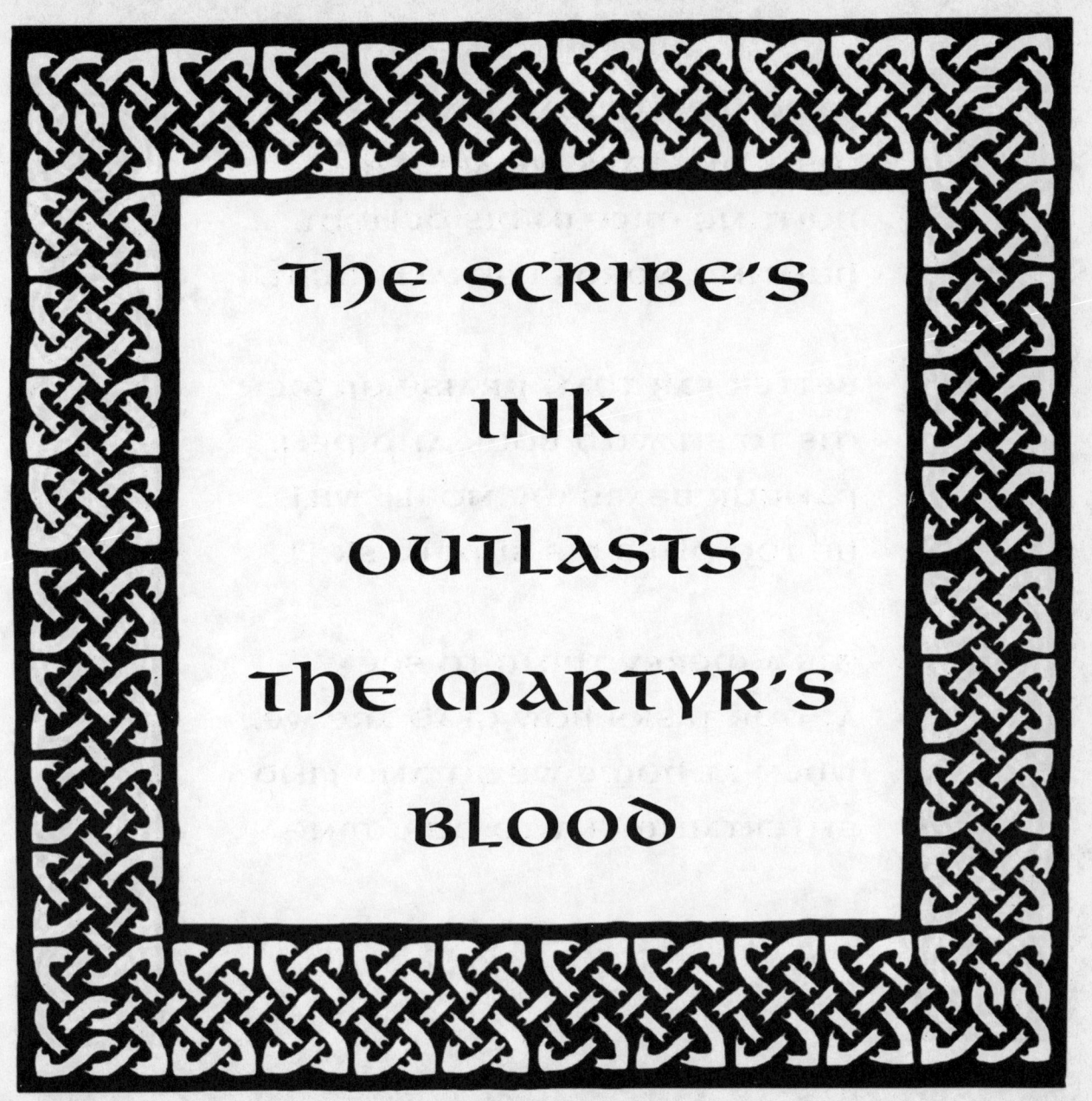

THE SCRIBE'S

INK

OUTLASTS

THE MARTYR'S

BLOOD

I AND PANGUR BAN MY CAT,
'TIS A LIKE TASK WE ARE AT:
HUNTING MICE IN HIS DELIGHT,
HUNTING WORDS I SIT ALL NIGHT.

BETTER FAR THAN PRAISE OF MEN
'TIS TO SIT WITH BOOK AND PEN:
PANGUR BEARS ME NO ILL WILL,
HE TOO PLIES HIS SIMPLE SKILL.

'TIS A MERRY THING TO SEE
AT OUR TASKS HOW GLAD ARE WE,
WHEN AT HOME WE SIT AND FIND
ENTERTAINMENT TO OUR MIND.

OFTENTIMES A MOUSE WILL STRAY
IN THE HERO PANGUR'S WAY:
OFTENTIMES MY KEEN THOUGHT SET
TAKES A MEANING IN ITS NET.

SO IN PEACE OUR TASKS WE PLY,
PANGUR BAN, MY CAT, AND I.
IN OUR ARTS WE FIND BLISS,
I HAVE MINE AND HE HAS HIS.

PRACTICE EVERY DAY HAS MADE
PANGUR PERFECT IN HIS TRADE.
I GET WISDOM DAY AND NIGHT
TURNING DARKNESS INTO LIGHT.

Written in Irish as a footnote to a manuscript now preserved
in the Benedictine monastery of St Paul, Carinthia, Austria.

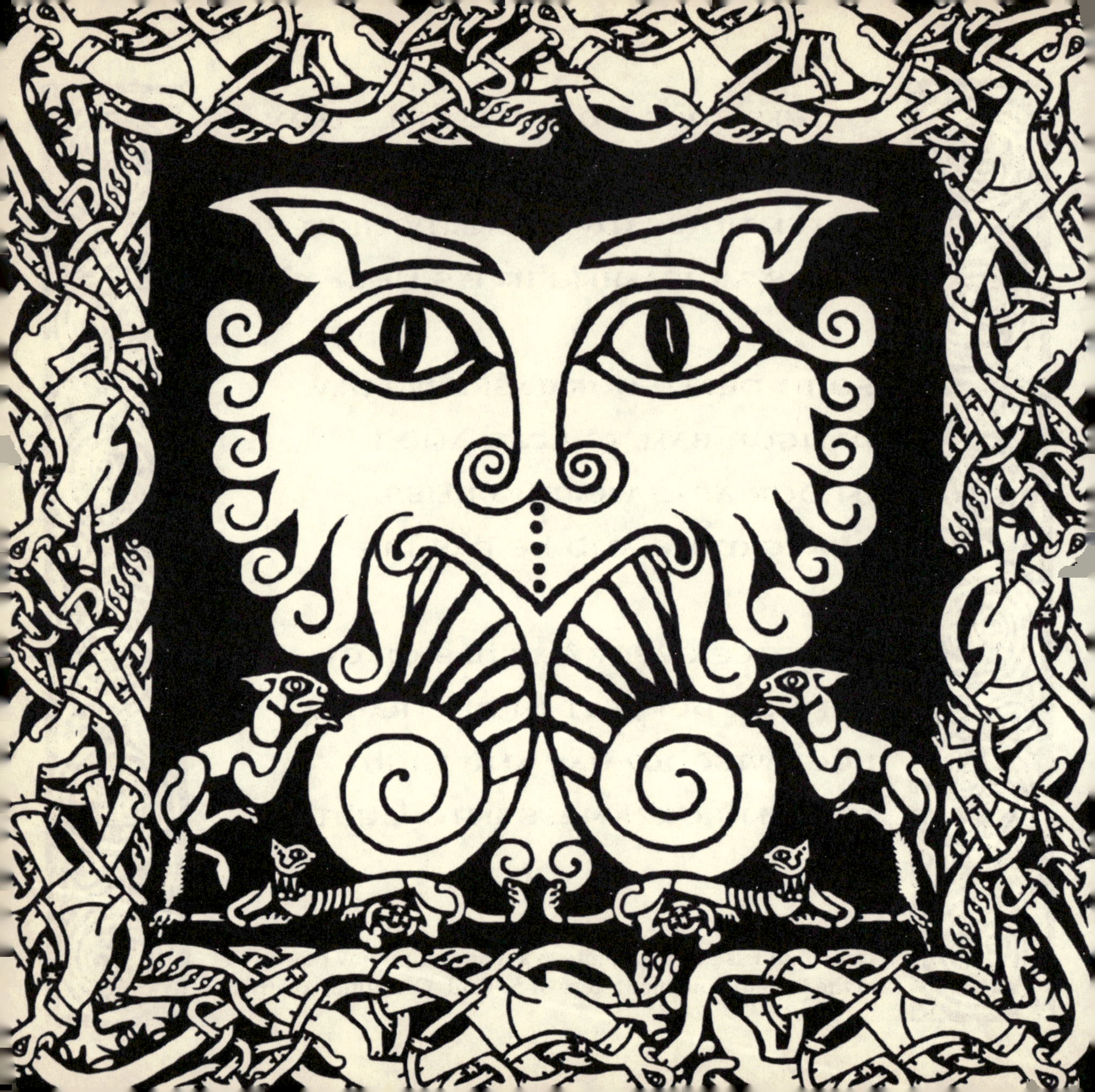

CONSIDER

CONCEIVE

CONCENTRATE

CREATE

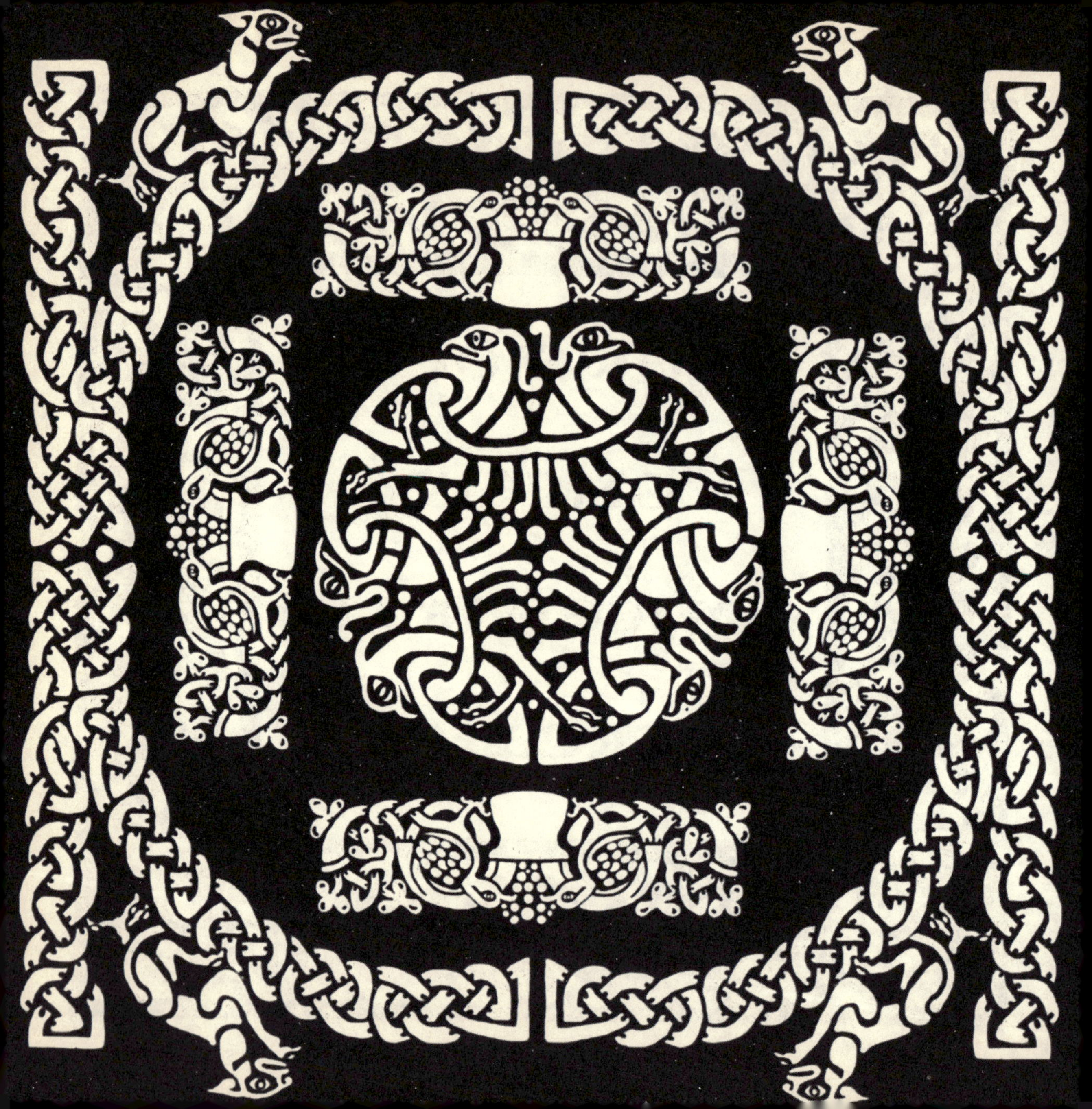

LOOK AT THEM SUPERFICIALLY WITH AN ORDINARY
CASUAL GLANCE, AND YOU WOULD MISS THE DETAIL.
FINE CRAFTSMANSHIP IS ALL ABOUT YOU, BUT YOU
MIGHT NOT NOTICE IT.

LOOK MORE KEENLY AT IT. YOU WILL MAKE OUT
INTRICACIES SO DELICATE AND SUBTLE, SO EXACT
AND COMPACT, SO FULL OF KNOTS AND LINKS AND
WITH COLOURS SO FRESH AND VIVID THAT YOU
MIGHT SAY THAT ALL THIS WAS THE WORK OF
ANGELS AND NOT OF MEN.

FOR MY PART THE MORE OFTEN I SEE THE BOOK
AND THE MORE CAREFULLY I STUDY IT, THE MORE
I AM LOST IN AMAZEMENT, AND I SEE MORE
CLEARLY THE WONDERS OF THE PAGES.

Giraldus Cambrensis (Gerald of Wales) from his twelfth century
travel book *Topographia Hiberniae*. This is believed to be a
description of *The Book of Kells*.

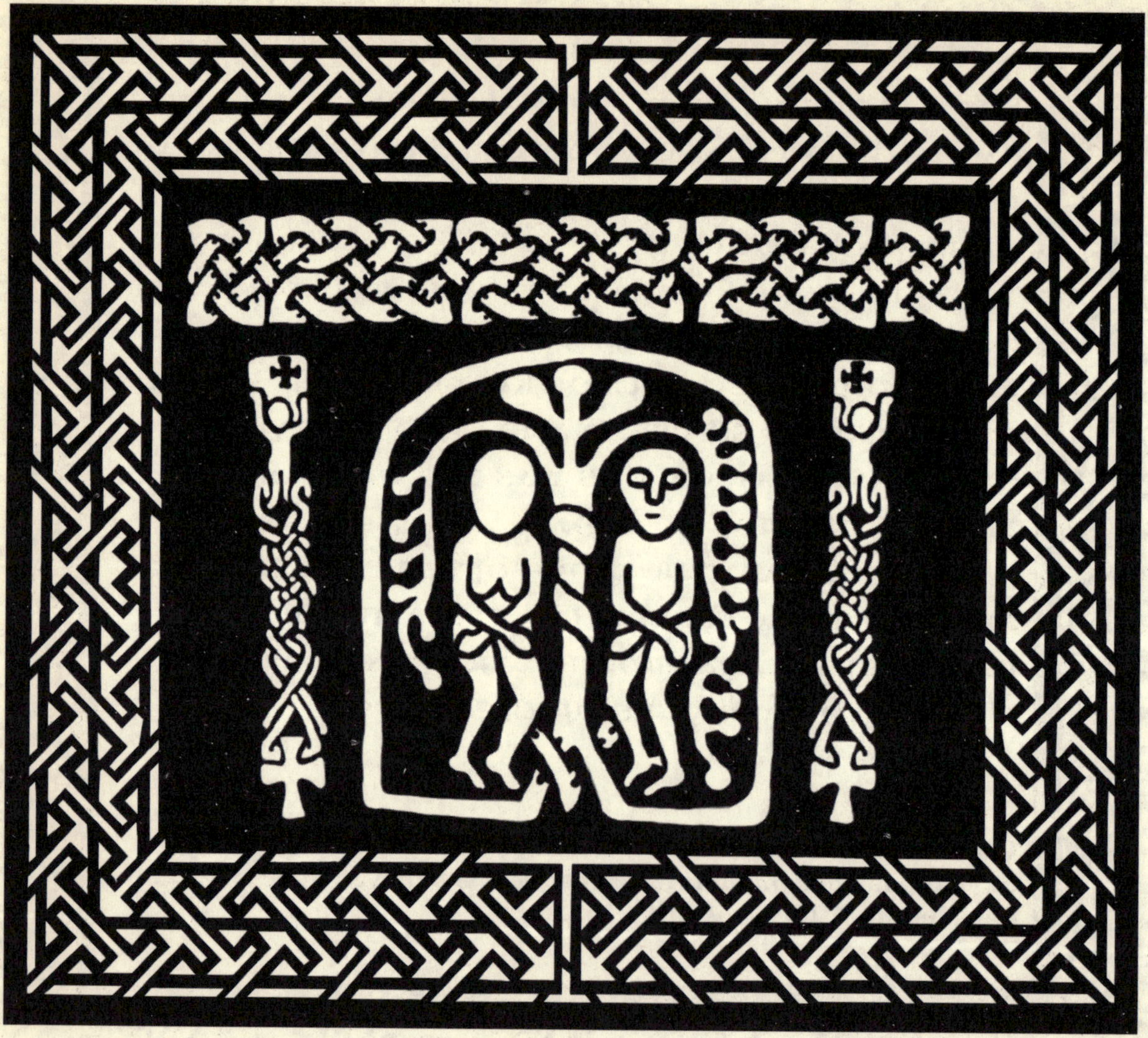

ADAM AND EVE

The Christian monks preserved many of the ancient stories of Ireland, but they often added touches that were peculiarly Christian. For example, all geneaologies began to include Adam and Eve, so that everyone could trace their ancestry back to biblical times rather than to pagan Gods. The story of Eve's temptation did not prove popular in a society where women had equal status to men and it was several centuries before even the Irish monks began to take the idea of original sin seriously.

THE MOUTH
THAT DOES
NOT
SPEAK
IS SWEET TO
LISTEN TO

I MANAGE VERY WELL ALL ALONE. THE WORLD IS MY FRIEND. SATISFACTION COMES FROM THE LIFE OF A HERMIT. UNEXPECTED ENCOUNTERS ARE JUST GOD'S WILL UNFOLDING. THEY ARE A JOURNEY IN TRUST. SOLITUDE IS A POWERFUL TEACHER.

An old man I met in Donegal in 1984.

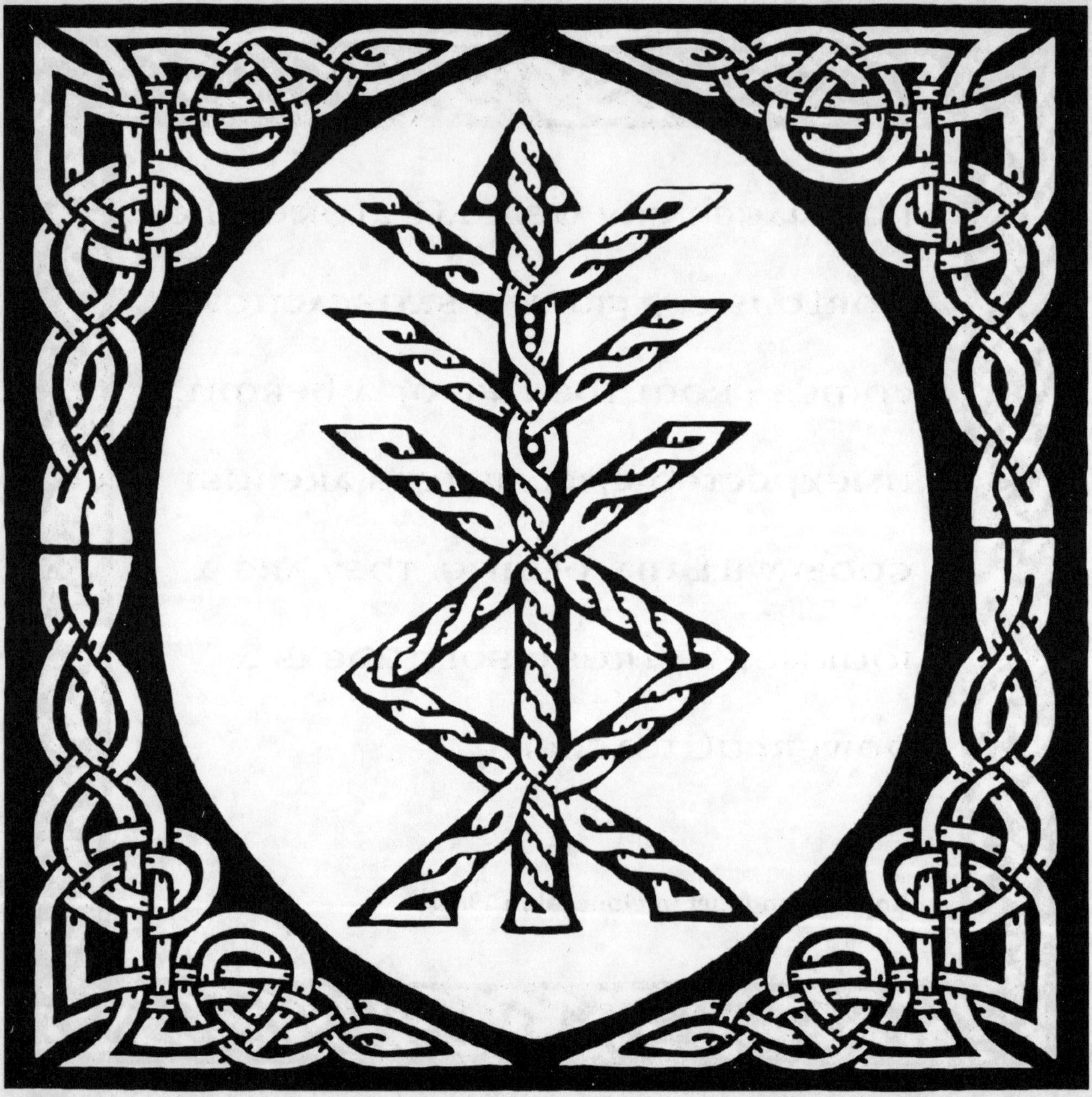

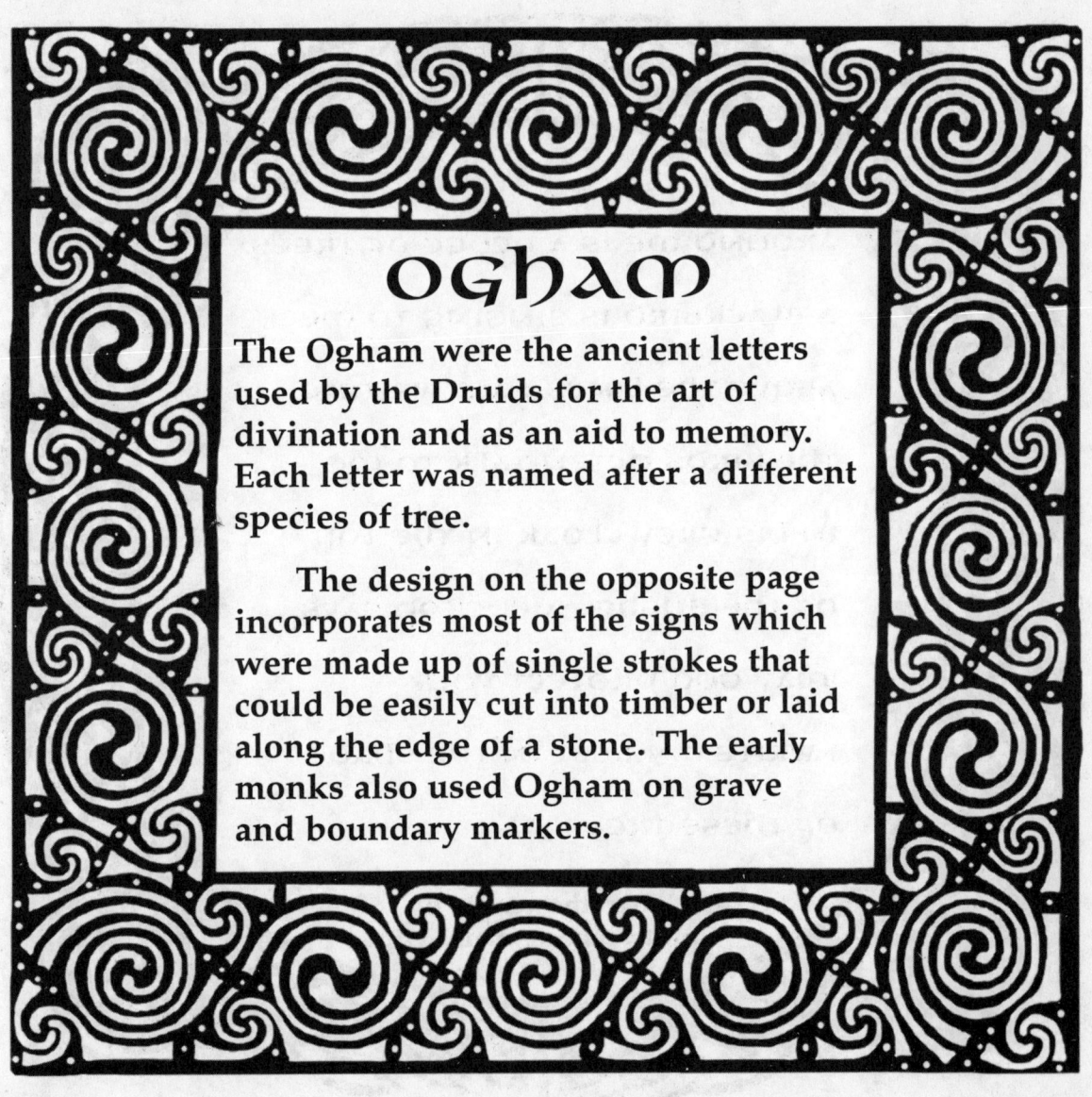

Ogham

The Ogham were the ancient letters used by the Druids for the art of divination and as an aid to memory. Each letter was named after a different species of tree.

The design on the opposite page incorporates most of the signs which were made up of single strokes that could be easily cut into timber or laid along the edge of a stone. The early monks also used Ogham on grave and boundary markers.

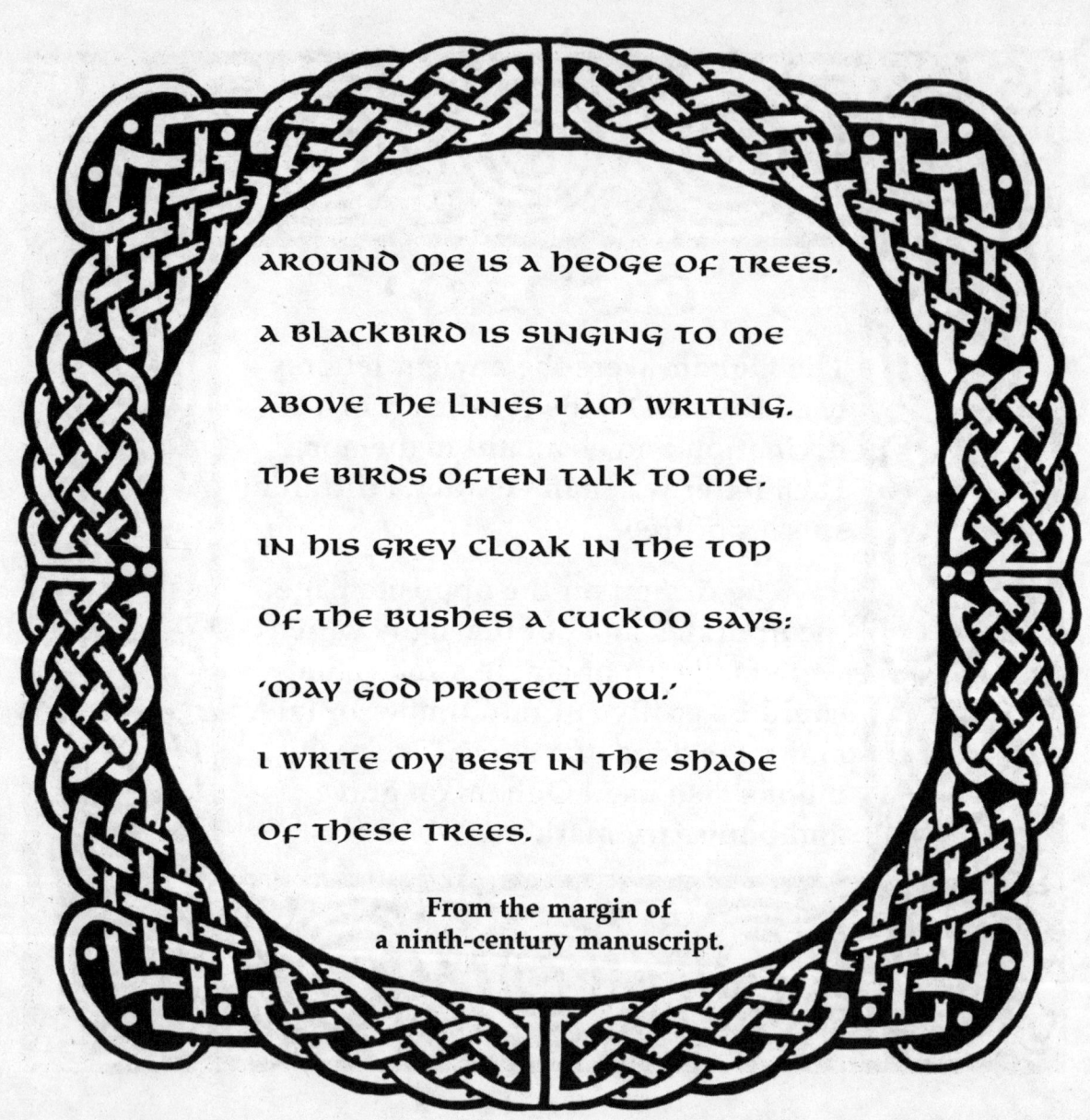

AROUND ME IS A HEDGE OF TREES.

A BLACKBIRD IS SINGING TO ME

ABOVE THE LINES I AM WRITING.

THE BIRDS OFTEN TALK TO ME.

IN HIS GREY CLOAK IN THE TOP

OF THE BUSHES A CUCKOO SAYS:

'MAY GOD PROTECT YOU.'

I WRITE MY BEST IN THE SHADE

OF THESE TREES.

From the margin of
a ninth-century manuscript.

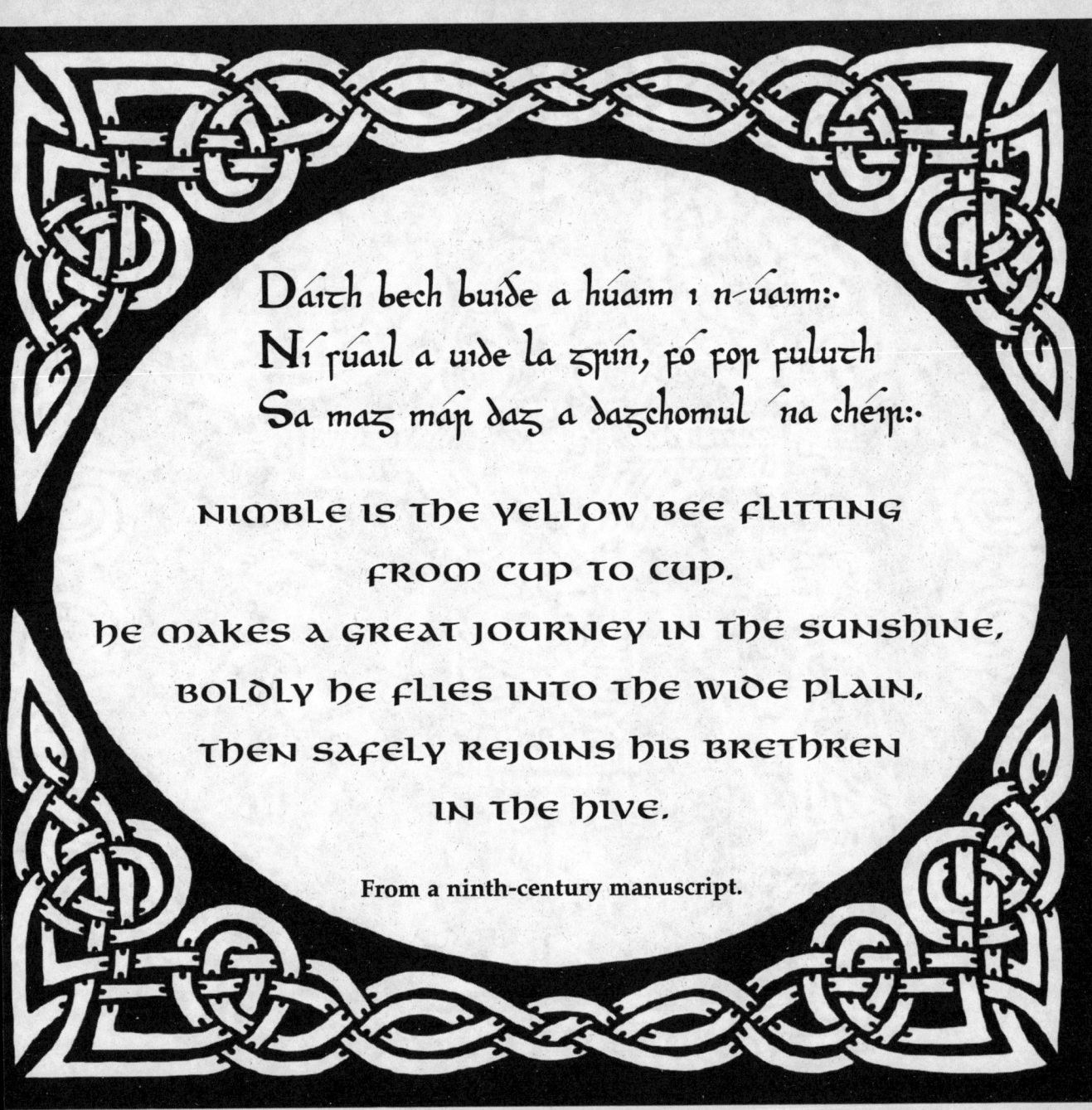

Dáith bech buide a húaim i n-úaim:·

Ní ruail a uide la ɣrín, fó for fuluth

Sa maɣ máp daɣ a daɣchomul ´na chéip:·

NIMBLE IS THE YELLOW BEE FLITTING

FROM CUP TO CUP.

HE MAKES A GREAT JOURNEY IN THE SUNSHINE,

BOLDLY HE FLIES INTO THE WIDE PLAIN,

THEN SAFELY REJOINS HIS BRETHREN

IN THE HIVE.

From a ninth-century manuscript.

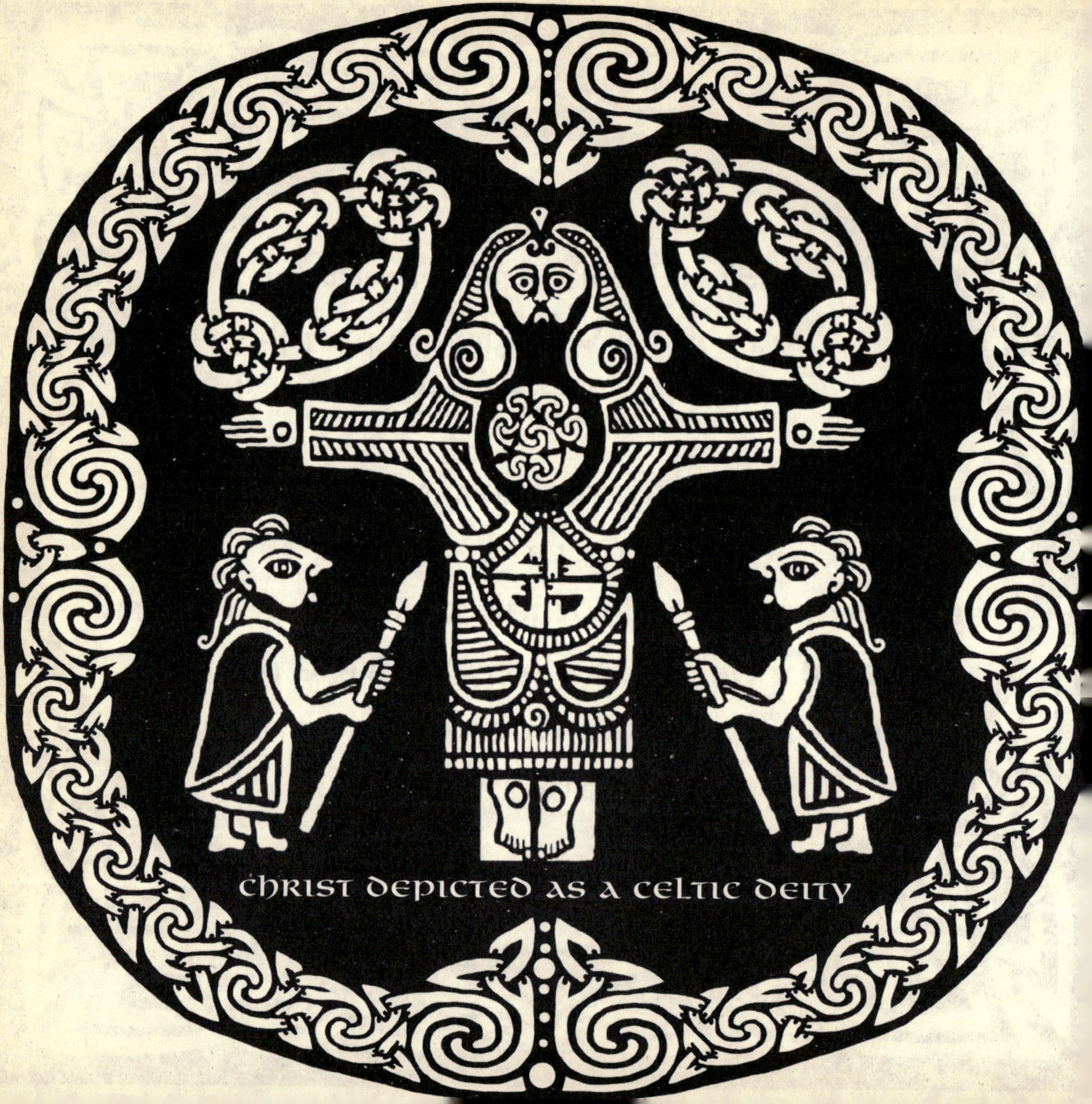

Christ depicted as a Celtic deity

the celtic christ

Whenever the early Christian monks wrote about Christ they were careful to emphasise the heroic elements of the tale, knowing that the Irish would listen more attentively if they could relate the exploits of the new God to those of the Old Gods. The scribes' depictions of Christ and the saints stared directly at the viewer, in much the same manner as the carvings of pre-Christian idols. Even the warriors who stand to either side of Christ on the opposite page have a very Celtic look about them, probably because Roman soldiers were unknown in Ireland and the north of Scotland.

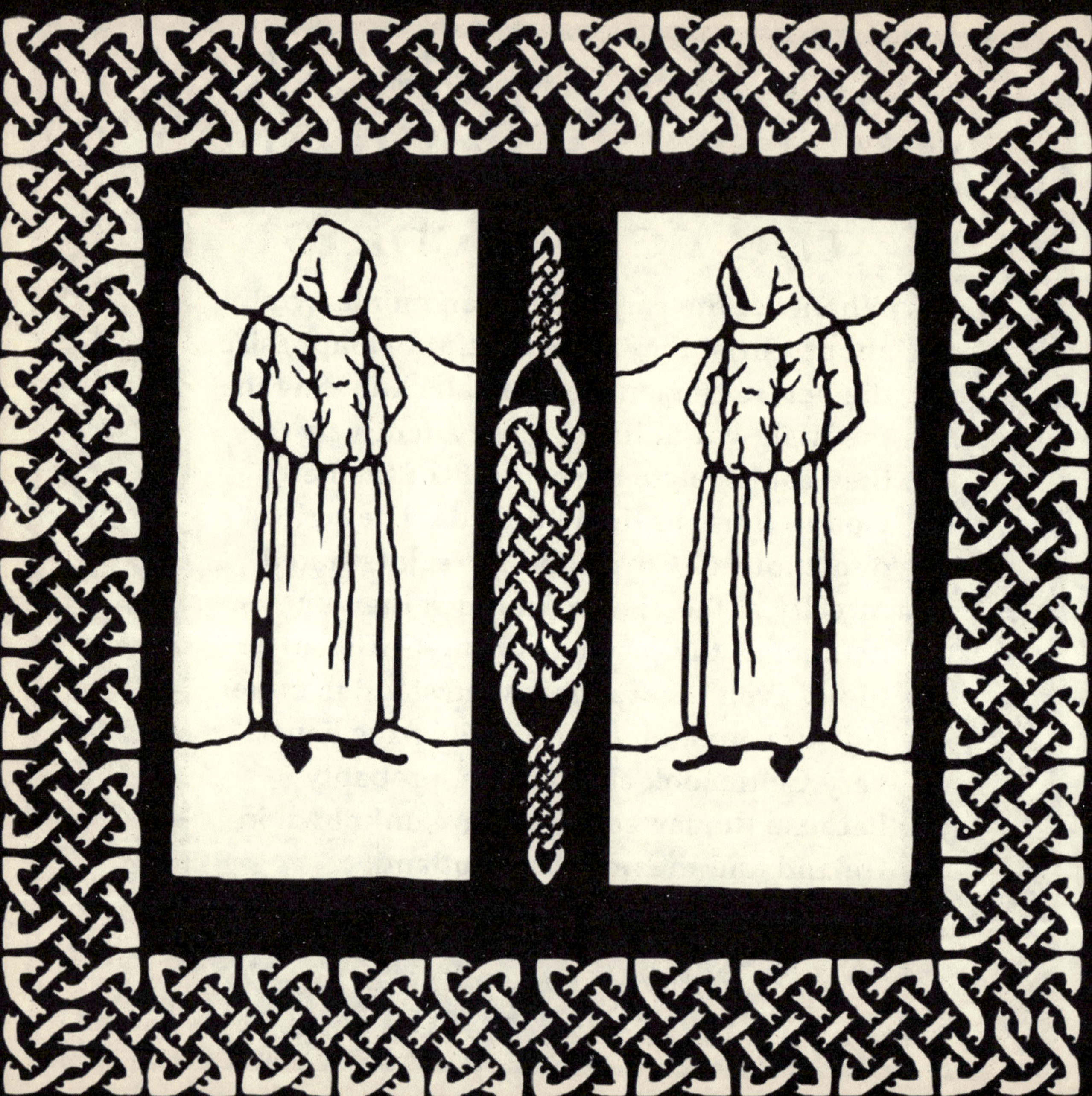

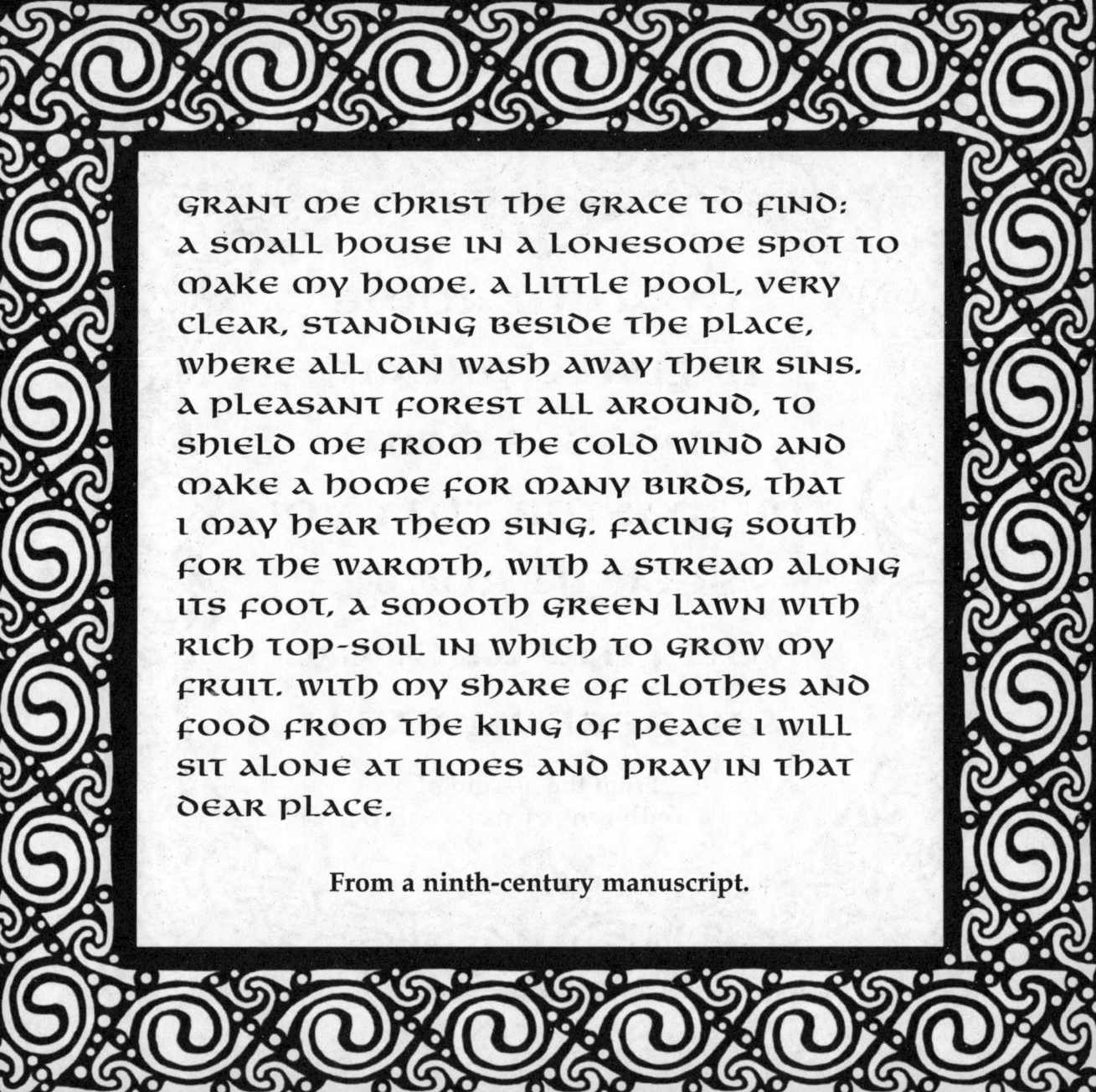

GRANT ME CHRIST THE GRACE TO FIND;
A SMALL HOUSE IN A LONESOME SPOT TO
MAKE MY HOME. A LITTLE POOL, VERY
CLEAR, STANDING BESIDE THE PLACE,
WHERE ALL CAN WASH AWAY THEIR SINS.
A PLEASANT FOREST ALL AROUND, TO
SHIELD ME FROM THE COLD WIND AND
MAKE A HOME FOR MANY BIRDS, THAT
I MAY HEAR THEM SING. FACING SOUTH
FOR THE WARMTH, WITH A STREAM ALONG
ITS FOOT, A SMOOTH GREEN LAWN WITH
RICH TOP-SOIL IN WHICH TO GROW MY
FRUIT. WITH MY SHARE OF CLOTHES AND
FOOD FROM THE KING OF PEACE I WILL
SIT ALONE AT TIMES AND PRAY IN THAT
DEAR PLACE.

From a ninth-century manuscript.

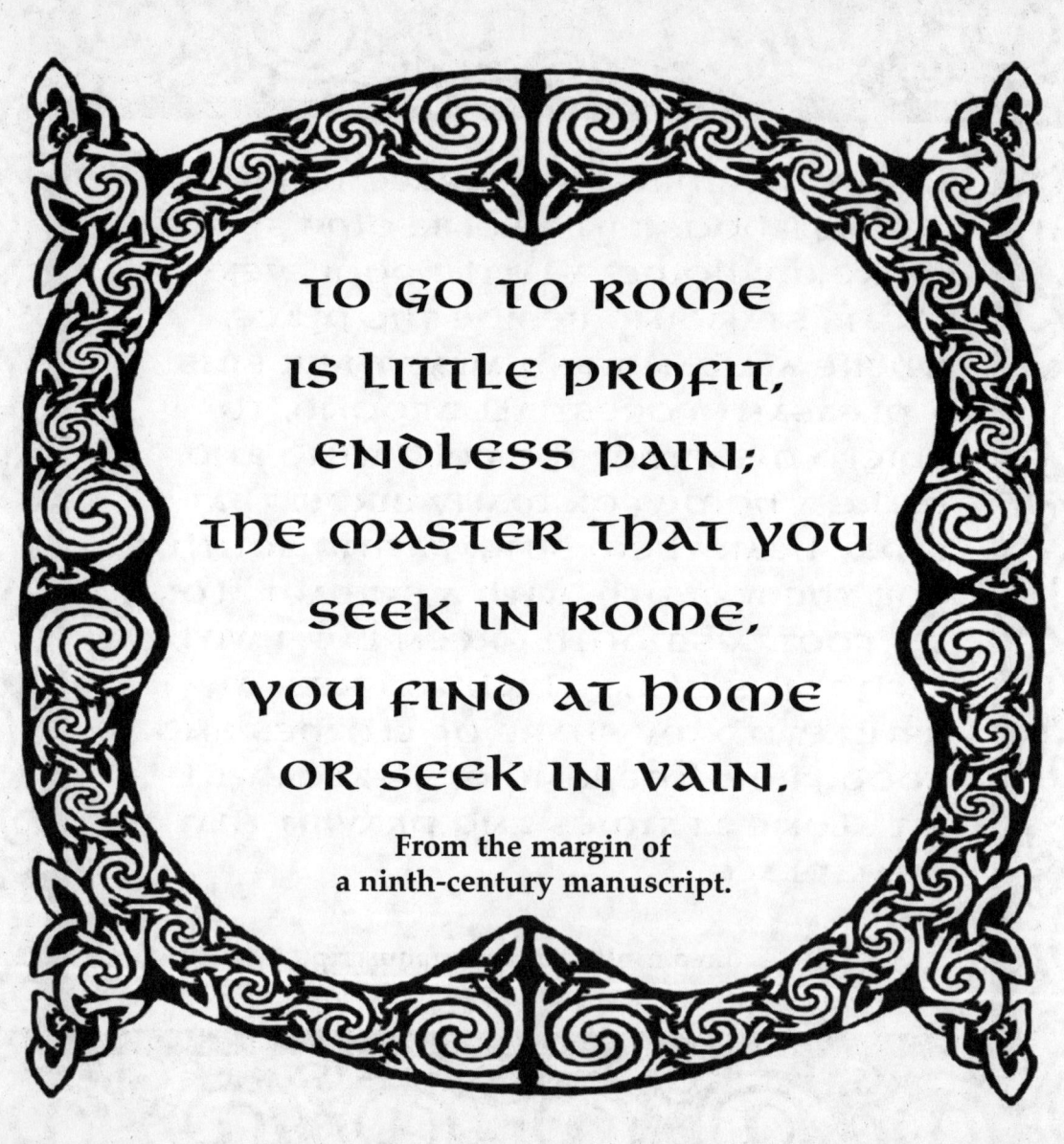

TO GO TO ROME
IS LITTLE PROFIT,
ENDLESS PAIN;
THE MASTER THAT YOU
SEEK IN ROME,
YOU FIND AT HOME
OR SEEK IN VAIN.

From the margin of
a ninth-century manuscript.

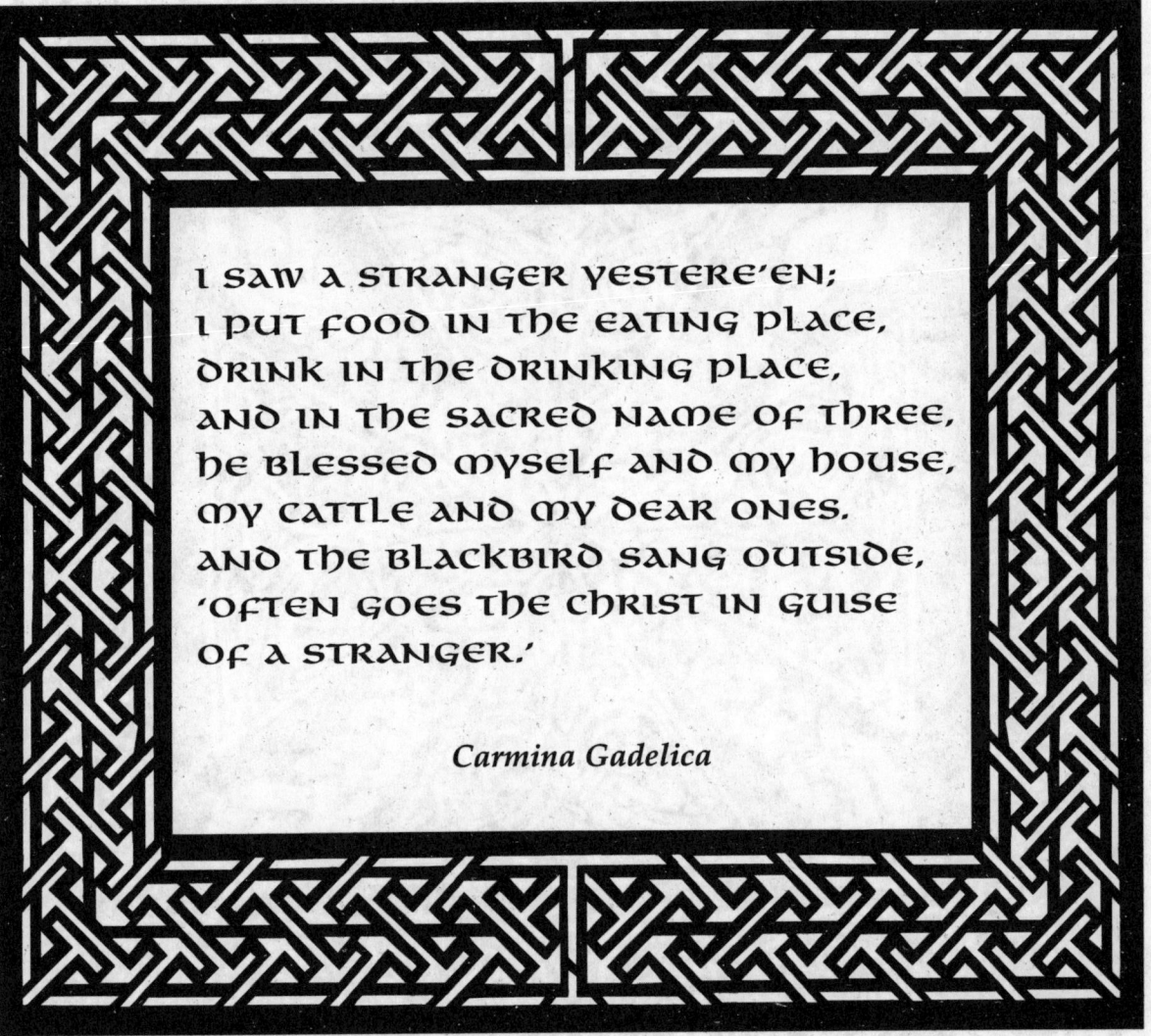

I SAW A STRANGER YESTERE'EN;
I PUT FOOD IN THE EATING PLACE,
DRINK IN THE DRINKING PLACE,
AND IN THE SACRED NAME OF THREE,
HE BLESSED MYSELF AND MY HOUSE,
MY CATTLE AND MY DEAR ONES.
AND THE BLACKBIRD SANG OUTSIDE,
'OFTEN GOES THE CHRIST IN GUISE
OF A STRANGER.'

Carmina Gadelica

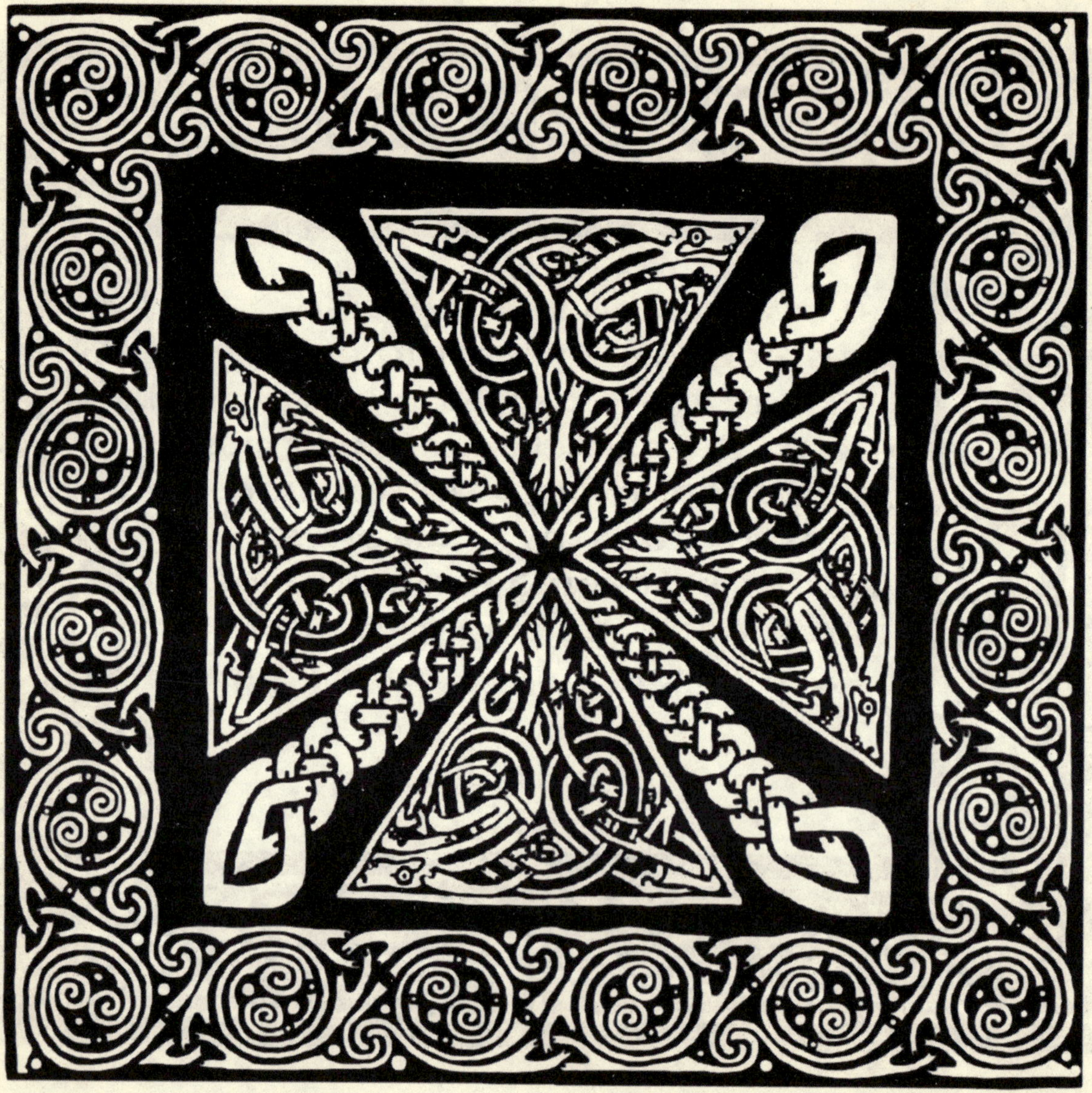

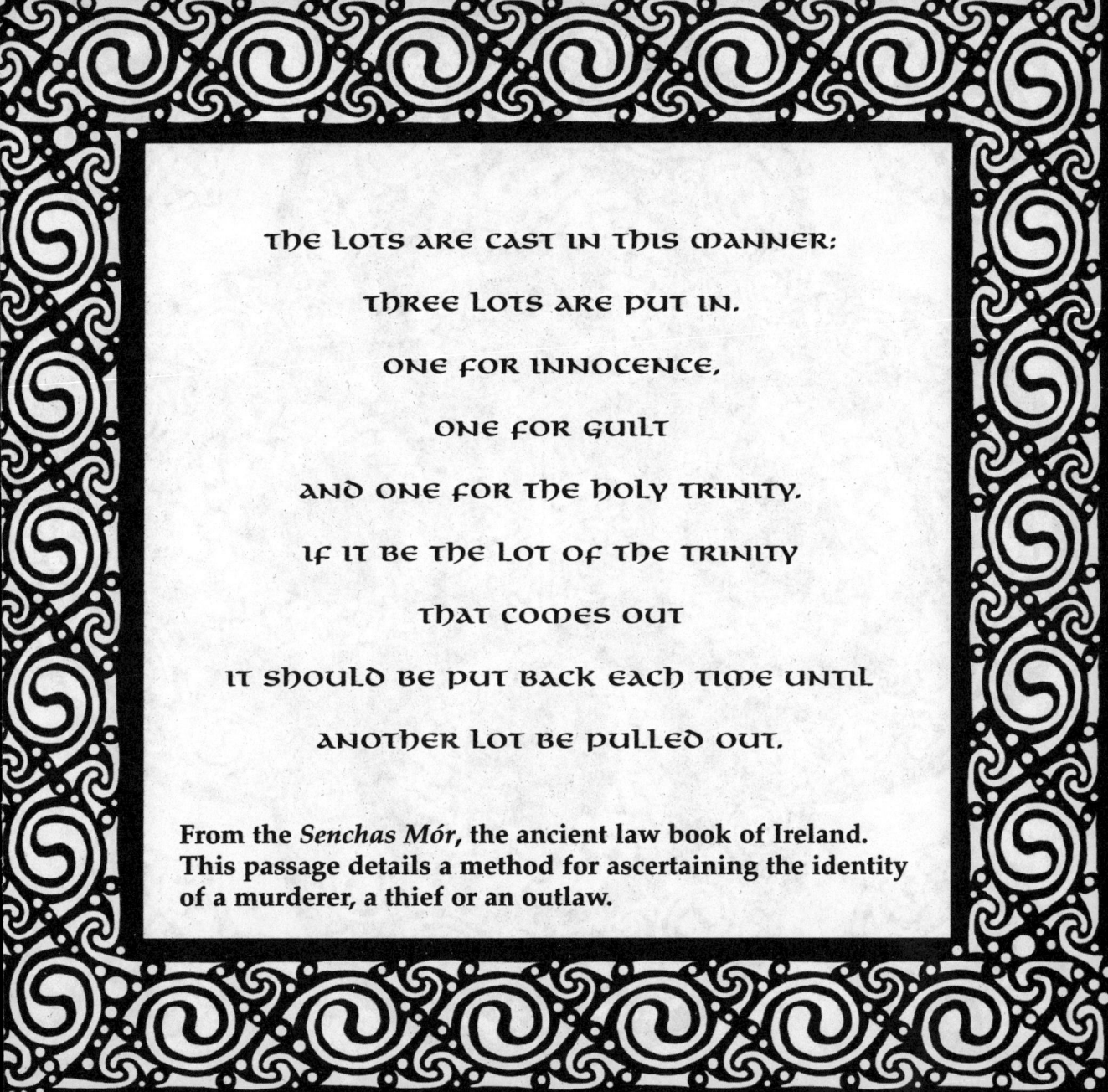

THE LOTS ARE CAST IN THIS MANNER:

THREE LOTS ARE PUT IN.

ONE FOR INNOCENCE,

ONE FOR GUILT

AND ONE FOR THE HOLY TRINITY.

IF IT BE THE LOT OF THE TRINITY

THAT COMES OUT

IT SHOULD BE PUT BACK EACH TIME UNTIL

ANOTHER LOT BE PULLED OUT.

From the *Senchas Mór*, the ancient law book of Ireland. This passage details a method for ascertaining the identity of a murderer, a thief or an outlaw.

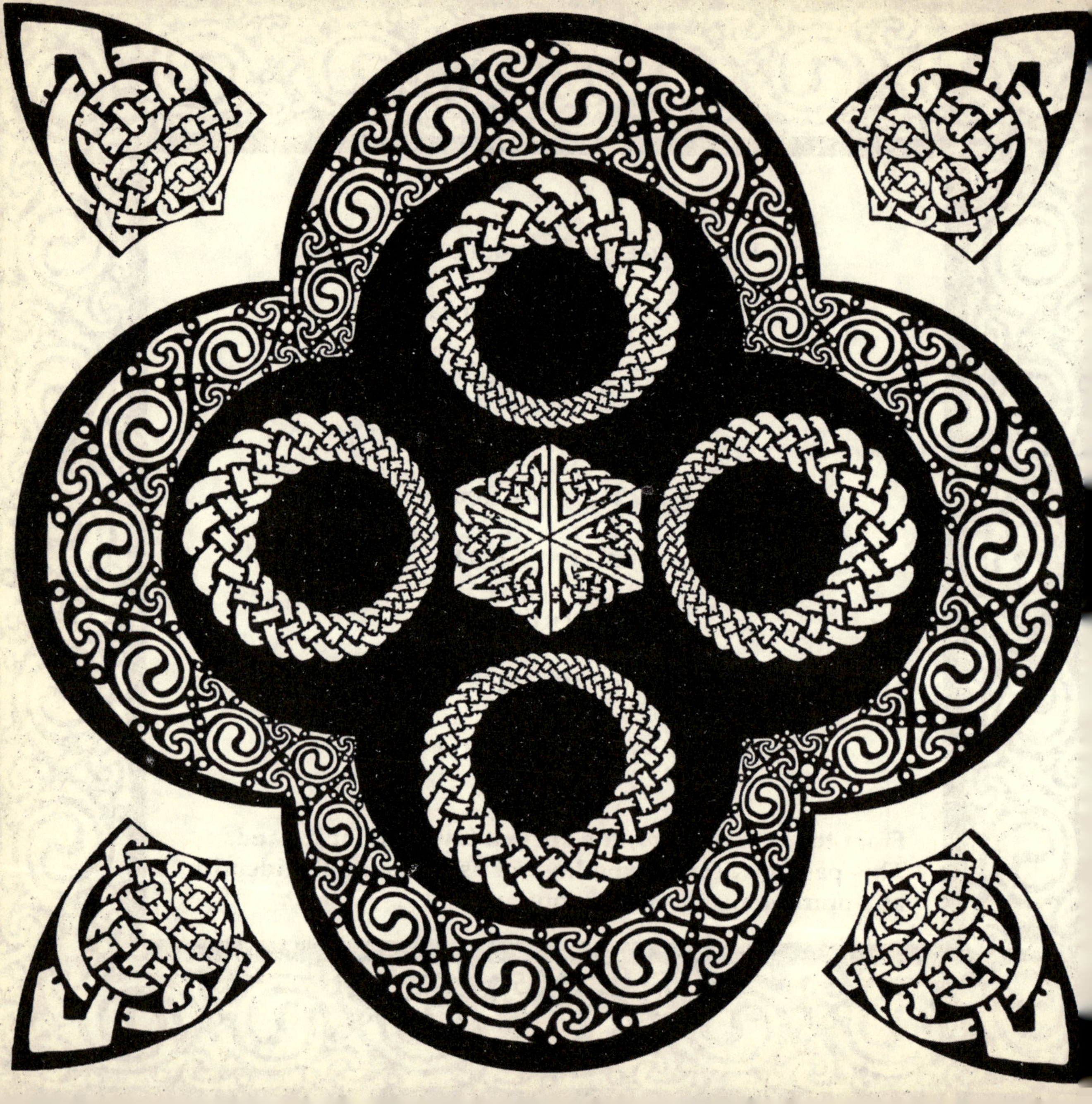

THE BLESSING OF GOD UPON YOU ALL,

MEN OF ERINN, SONS, WOMEN, AND DAUGHTERS;

PRINCE BLESSING, MEAL BLESSING,

BLESSINGS OF EXCELLENCE,

ETERNAL BLESSING, HEAVEN BLESSING,

CLOUD BLESSING, SEA BLESSING,

FRUIT BLESSING, LAND BLESSING,

CROP BLESSING, DEW BLESSING,

BLESSING OF THE ELEMENTS, BLESSING OF VALOUR,

BLESSING OF DEXTERITY, BLESSING OF GLORY,

BLESSING OF DEEDS, BLESSING OF HONOUR,

BLESSING OF HAPPINESS BE UPON YOU ALL,

LAITY, CLERICS, WHILE I COMMAND

THE BLESSING OF THE MEN OF HEAVEN;

IT IS MY BEQUEST, AS IT IS MY PERPETUAL BLESSING.

The blessing of Saint Patrick from the *Book of Rights*. This book was in fact compiled long before Patrick, but he was said to have been responsible for reviewing it. The book set out the rights and responsibilities of kings and chieftains in Ireland in the fifth century.

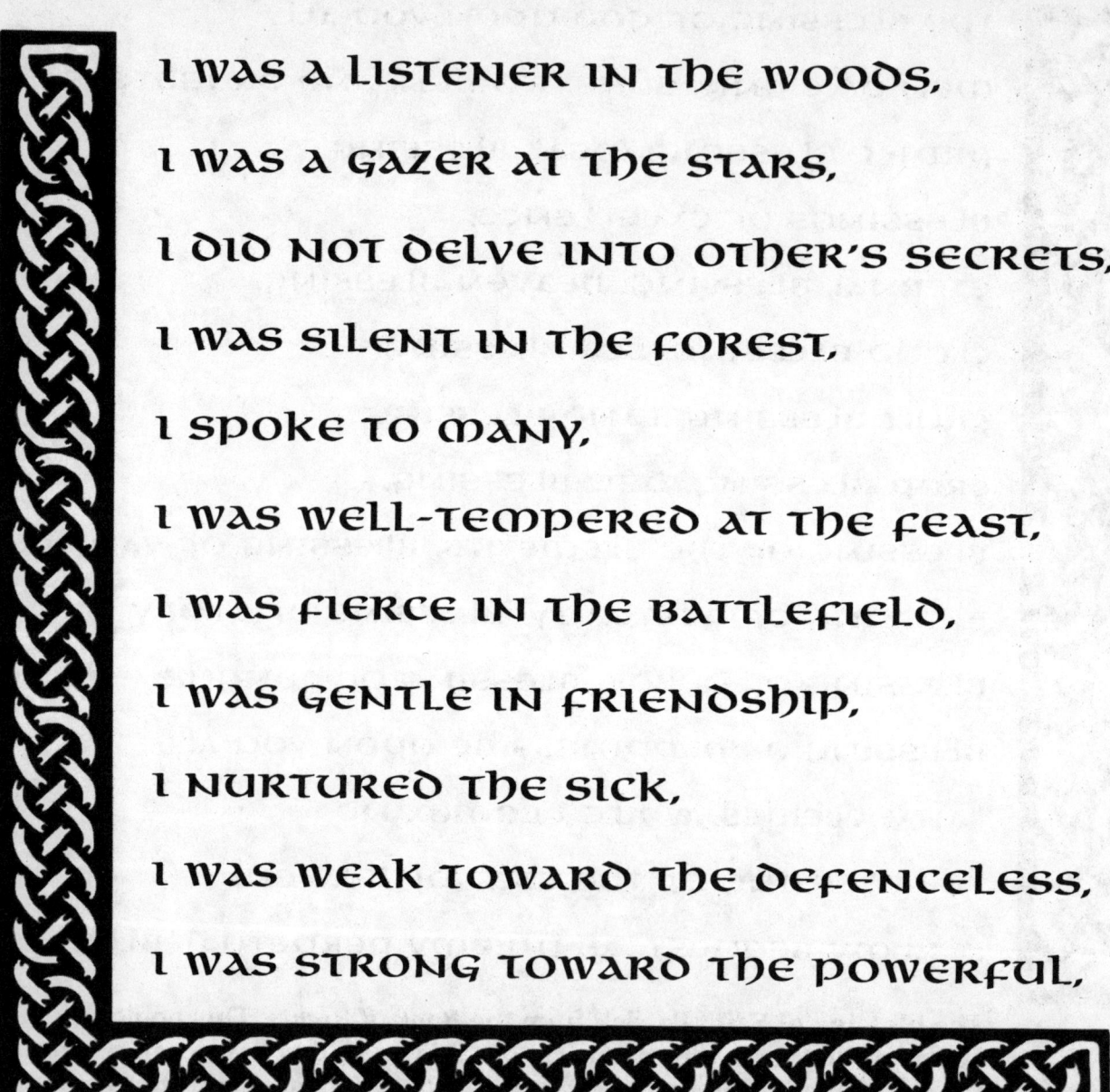

I WAS A LISTENER IN THE WOODS,

I WAS A GAZER AT THE STARS,

I DID NOT DELVE INTO OTHER'S SECRETS,

I WAS SILENT IN THE FOREST,

I SPOKE TO MANY,

I WAS WELL-TEMPERED AT THE FEAST,

I WAS FIERCE IN THE BATTLEFIELD,

I WAS GENTLE IN FRIENDSHIP,

I NURTURED THE SICK,

I WAS WEAK TOWARD THE DEFENCELESS,

I WAS STRONG TOWARD THE POWERFUL,

I WAS NOT ARROGANT
THOUGH I WAS WISE.
I DID NOT PROMISE TOO MUCH
THOUGH I WAS RICH.
I DID NOT BOAST
THOUGH I WAS SKILLED.
I DID NOT SPEAK ILL OF THOSE ABSENT.
I DID NOT REPRIMAND
BUT RATHER I WOULD PRAISE.
I DID NOT ASK, BUT I WOULD GIVE.

Cormac Mac Airt, High-King of Ireland, instructing his son, Cairbre, on life and kingship. From the *Leabhar Teagasc an Riogh* (the book of instructions for a king), sixth century.

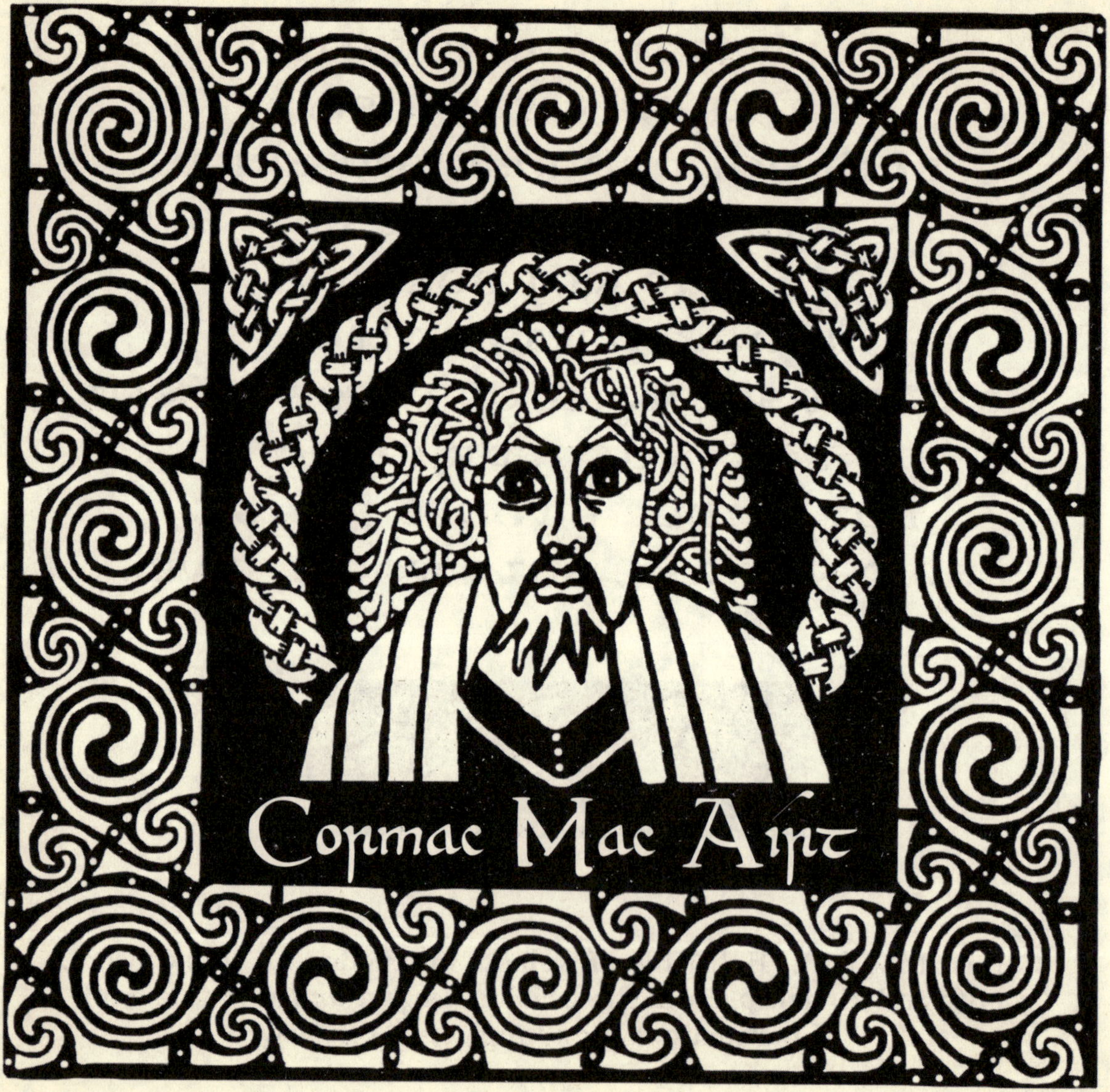
Cormac Mac Airt

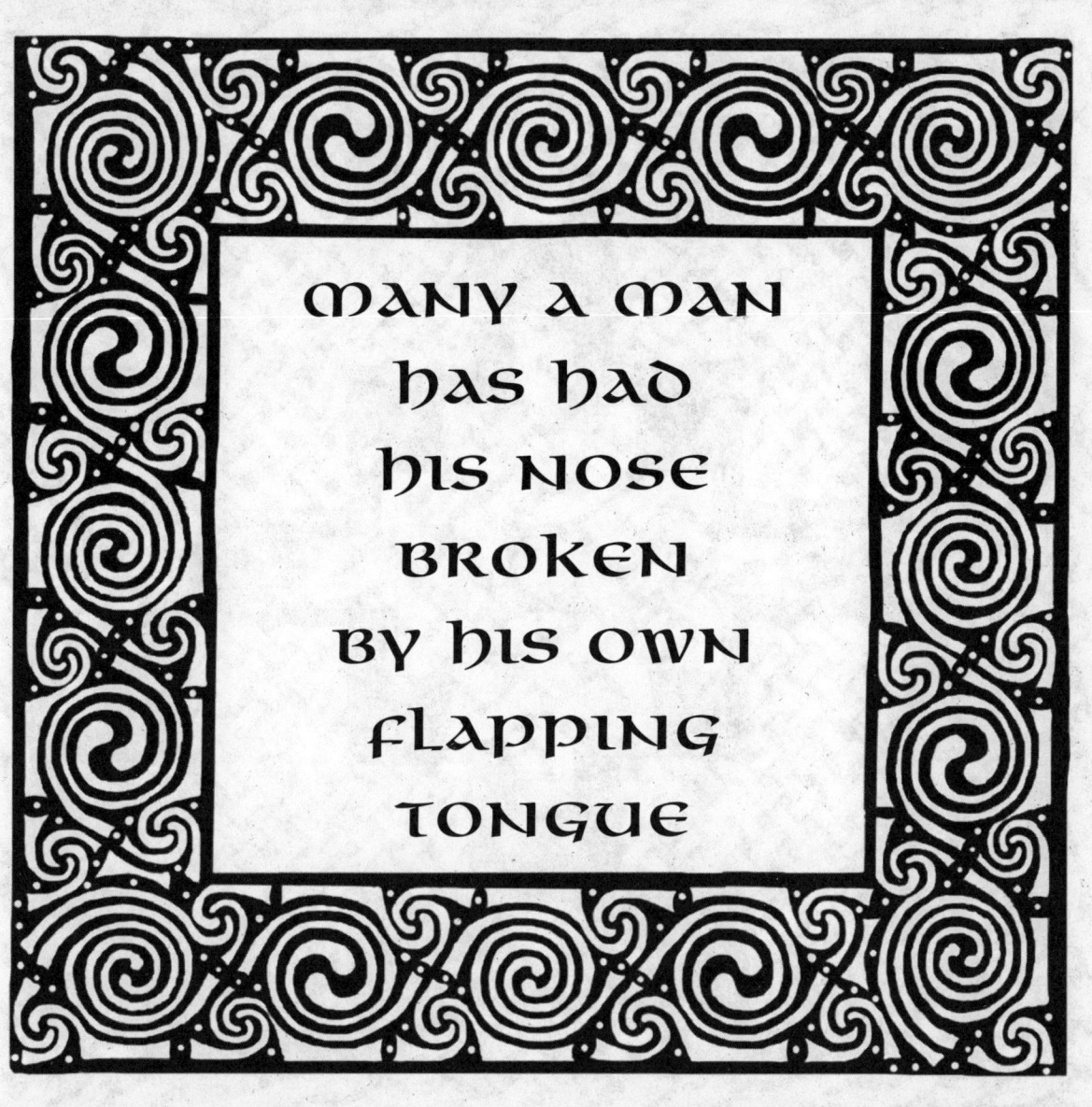

MANY A MAN
HAS HAD
HIS NOSE
BROKEN
BY HIS OWN
FLAPPING
TONGUE

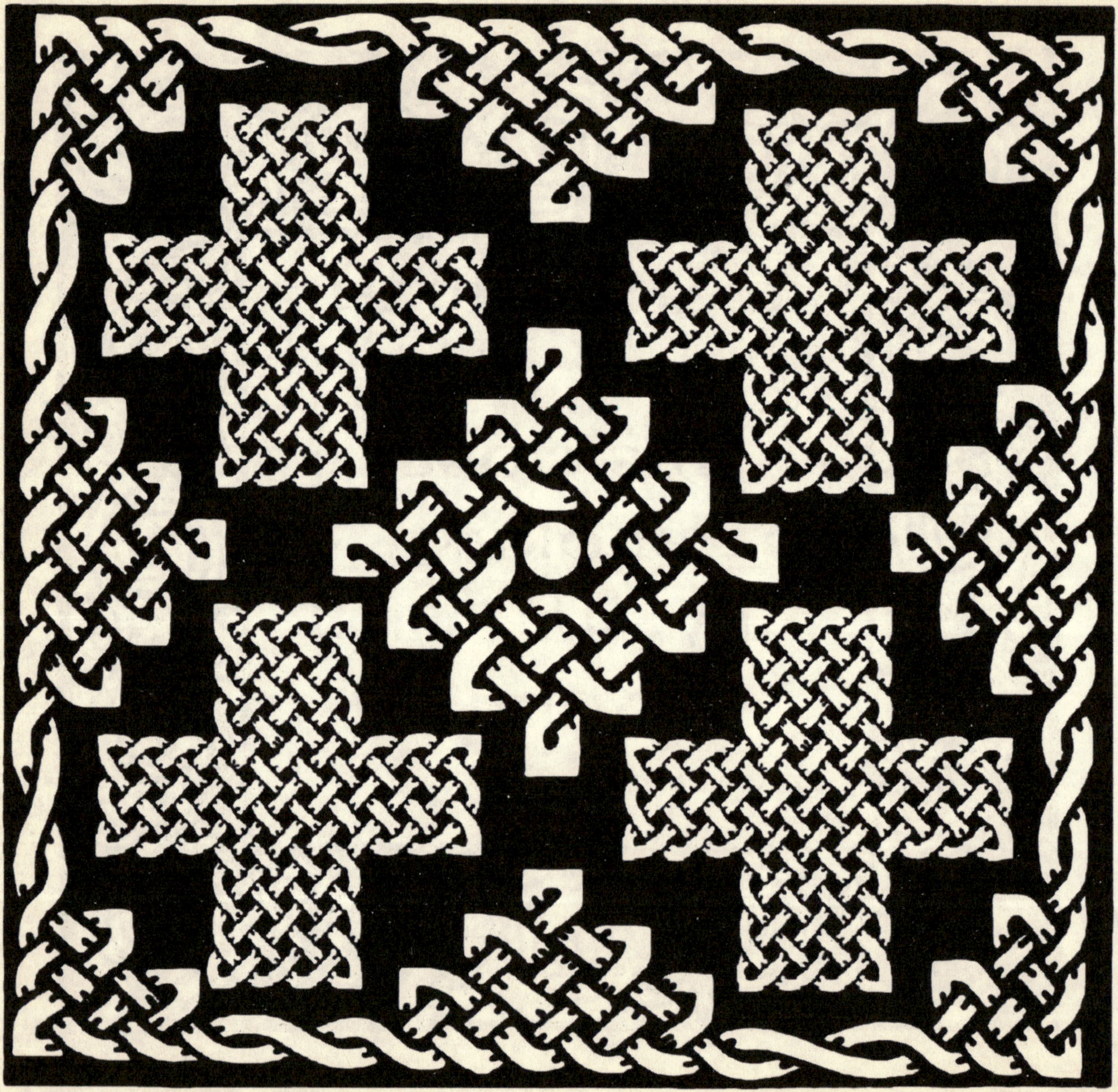

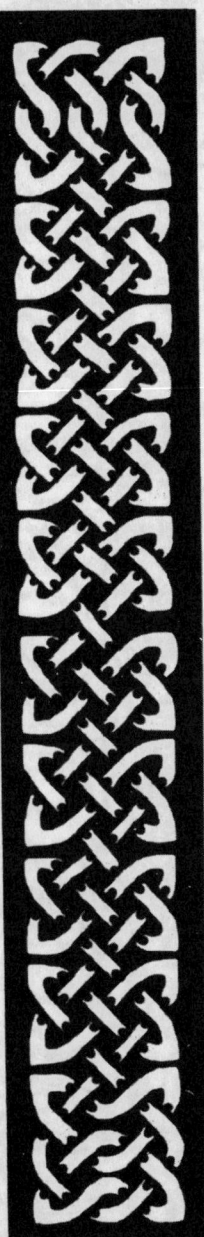

I WILL HAVE FAITH UNTIL THE SKY FALLS IN

AROUND ME AND CRUSHES ME;

UNTIL THE EARTH OPENS UP

AND SWALLOWS ME;

UNTIL THE SEAS RISE AND DROWN ME.

BE EACH SAINT IN HEAVEN,

EACH SAINTED WOMAN IN HEAVEN,

STRETCHING THEIR ARMS FOR YOU,

WHEN YOU GO THITHER OVER

THE RIVER HARD TO SEE;

WHEN YOU GO THITHER HOME

OVER THE RIVER HARD TO SEE.

Carmina Gadelica

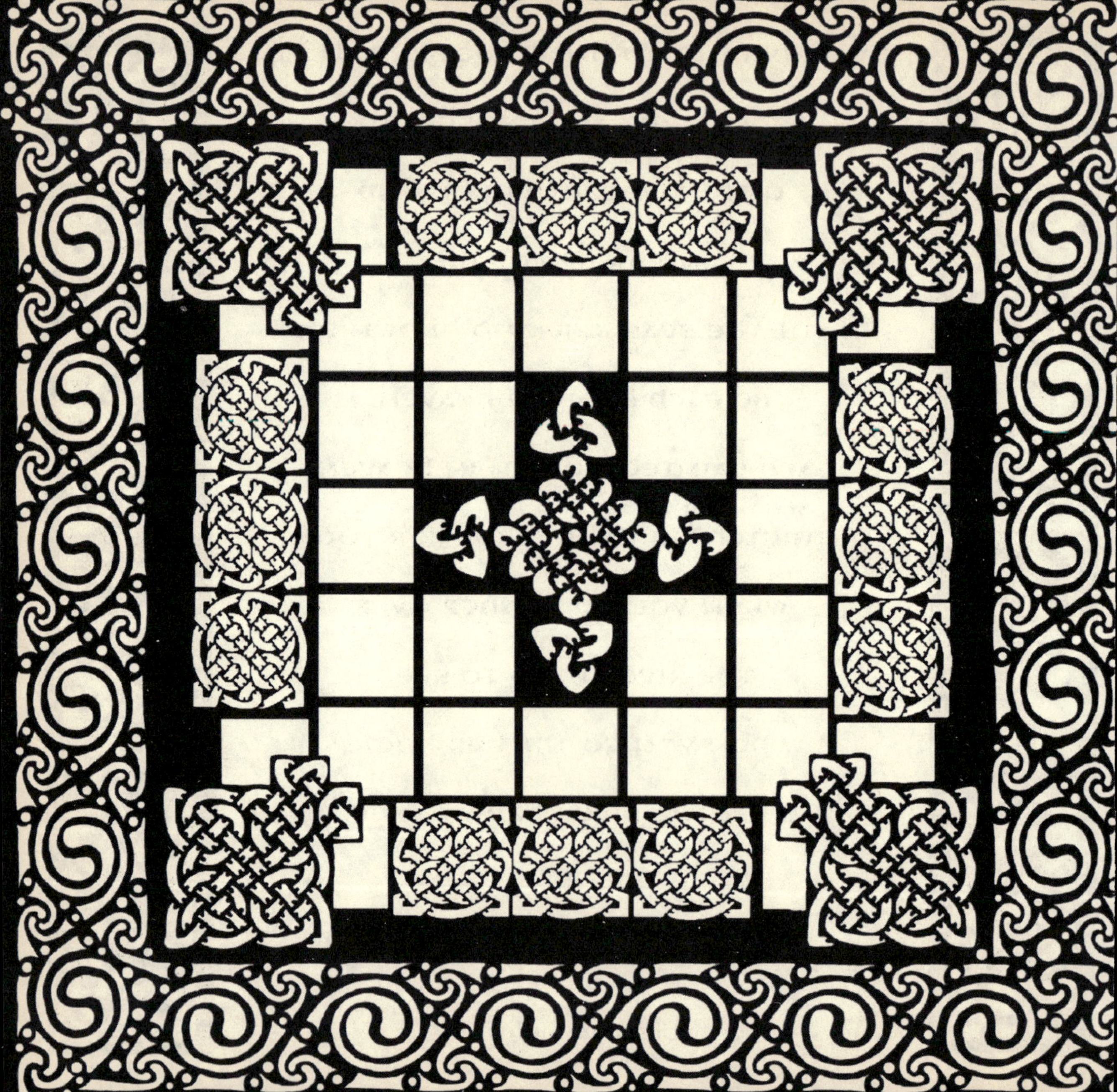

BRANDUBH

The Brandubh was an ancient game similar to chess which was very popular before Christianity reached Ireland. The opposite page shows what the board looked like. There were five white pieces and twelve black pieces. The white ones were set in the centre of the board and the black 'ravens' were set around the outside. The object of the game was for the white player to get his king past the ravens and into the sanctuary of one of the corners. The raven player had to surround the white king on all four sides to win the game.

   The Brandubh was much more than a game of skill, however. We know from the old tales that the board represented the land of Ireland with its four kingdoms. The white king stood for the High-King of Ireland who was elected by the other four kings as their overlord. As a test of his eligibility for the High-Kingship, a candidate had to play against the chief Druid of the land and win.

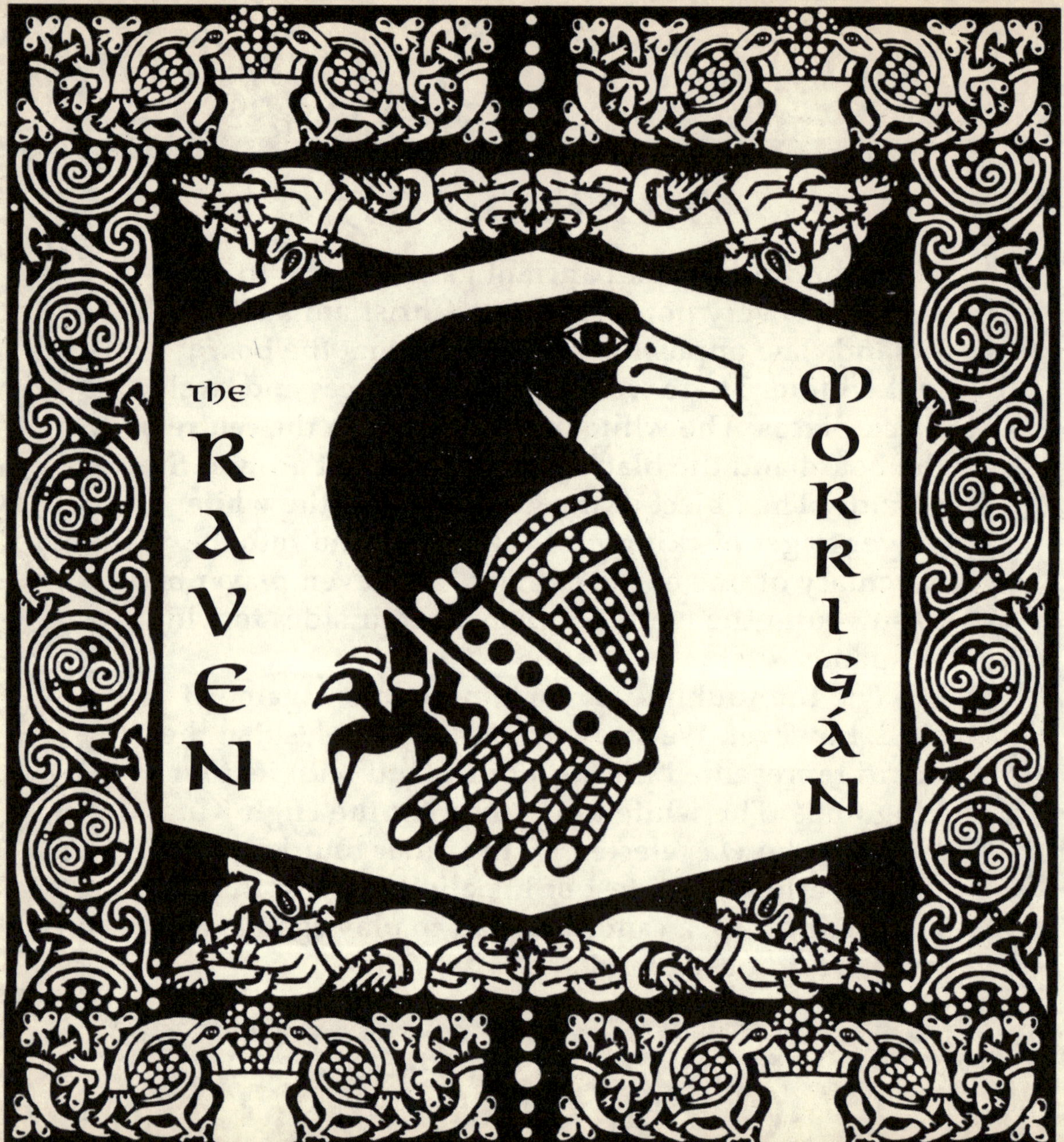
THE RAVEN
MORRIGÁN

Brandubh was an old Irish word for the raven. These birds symbolised the dark forces of the otherworld and the enemies that often assailed Ireland from beyond it shores. Ravens were considered to be the servants of the Morrigán, who took on the form of a carrion bird when she was the messenger of death. That is why the black pieces were known as ravens and how the Brandubh got its name.

The medieval monks copied down many stories which mention the Brandubh and left detailed descriptions of what the board looked like but the precise nature of the rules was lost. It seems that the game was so popular, even among the monks, that the Church was forced to outlaw it to prevent the brothers stealing off from services to play. Today one can still see rough game boards scratched into stone benches in ruined monasteries where the monks were supposed to sit and study the scriptures. Brandubh would have very likely been a welcome distraction in the hard life of a monk.

A MAN
WITH MANY
CATTLE
DOES NOT
SLEEP
EASY

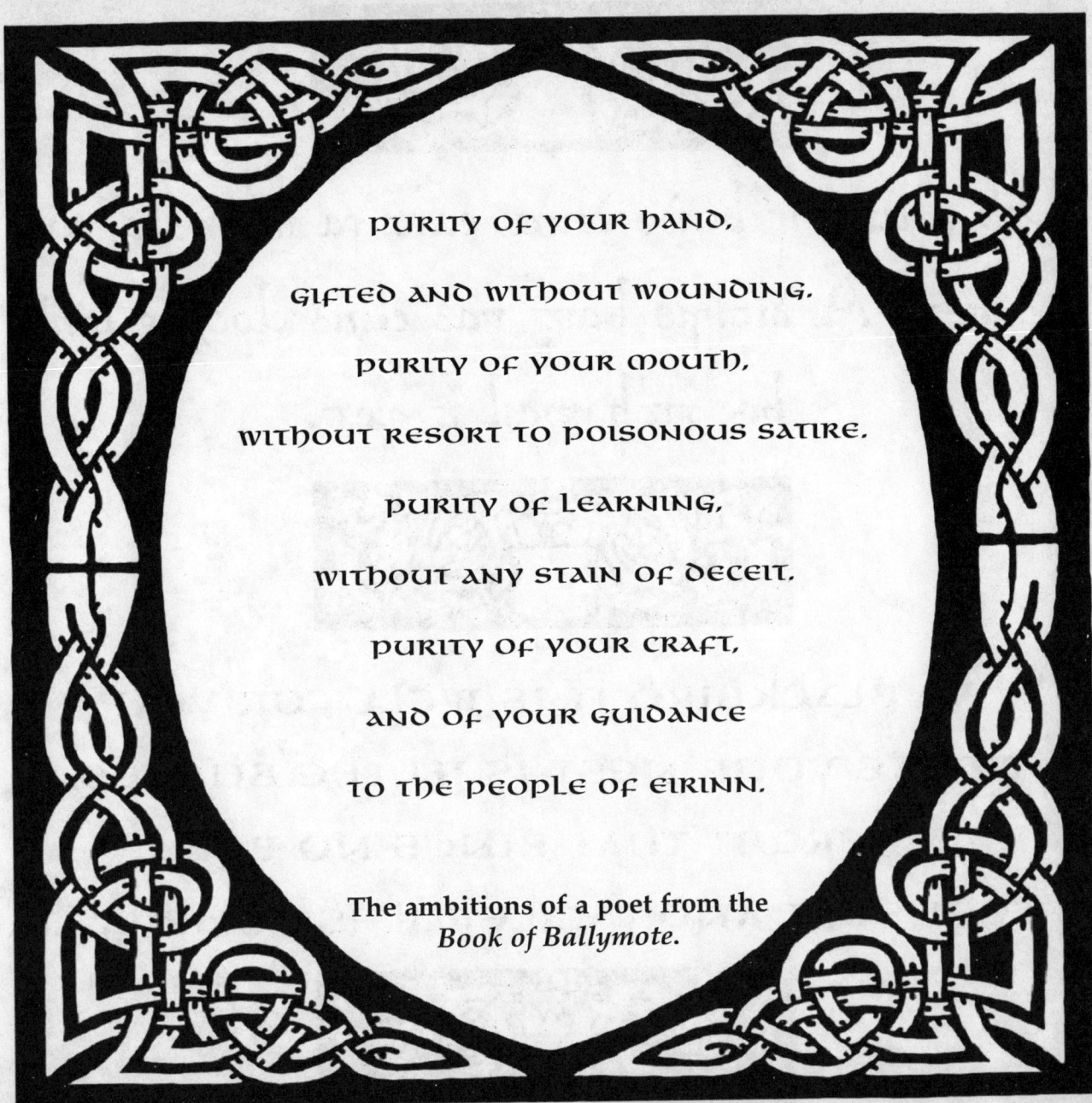

PURITY OF YOUR HAND,

GIFTED AND WITHOUT WOUNDING.

PURITY OF YOUR MOUTH,

WITHOUT RESORT TO POISONOUS SATIRE.

PURITY OF LEARNING,

WITHOUT ANY STAIN OF DECEIT,

PURITY OF YOUR CRAFT,

AND OF YOUR GUIDANCE

TO THE PEOPLE OF EIRINN.

The ambitions of a poet from the
Book of Ballymote.

Och a luin if buide duiτ, cáiτ ʃa muine a ʃuil
do neτ, A díτhʃe baiᵹ nad clind cloc, iʃ bind
boc ʃiτhamail τ ʃeτ.

ah BLACKBIRD IT IS WELL FOR YOU
WHERE YOUR NEST IS IN THE BUSHES,
a HERMIT THAT RINGS NO BELL,
SWEET SOFT AND PEACEFUL IS YOUR CALL.

SO, SINCE YOUR HEART IS SET ON HER SWEET GREEN FIELDS,

AND YOU WOULD LEAVE ME HERE,

GO QUICKLY, HEED NOT MY WORDS,

ALTHOUGH IT BE THE VOICE OF YOUR FRIEND.

YOU ARE CAPTURED BY THE LOVE OF YOUR OWN LAND.

WHO AM I TO HINDER LOVE?

WHY SHOULD I BLAME YOU FOR YOUR WEARINESS?

IF BUT CHRIST WOULD GIVE ME BACK THE YEARS,

AND THE STRENGTH OF MY YOUTH,

AND DARKEN THE WHITE HAIRS ON MY HEAD,

I WOULD GO WITH YOU.

THE WIDE SEAS THAT MUST BE CROSSED, TERRIFY ME;

BUT GO, MY SON, MAY YOUR SHIP CUT SWIFTLY

THROUGH THE WAVES, AND DO NOT QUITE FORGET.

This was written by Colman, a ninth-century Irish missionary who travelled through Europe spreading the Word to the Germans and Franks who had lapsed back into paganism. He was lamenting the departure of a good friend who was returning home to Ireland.

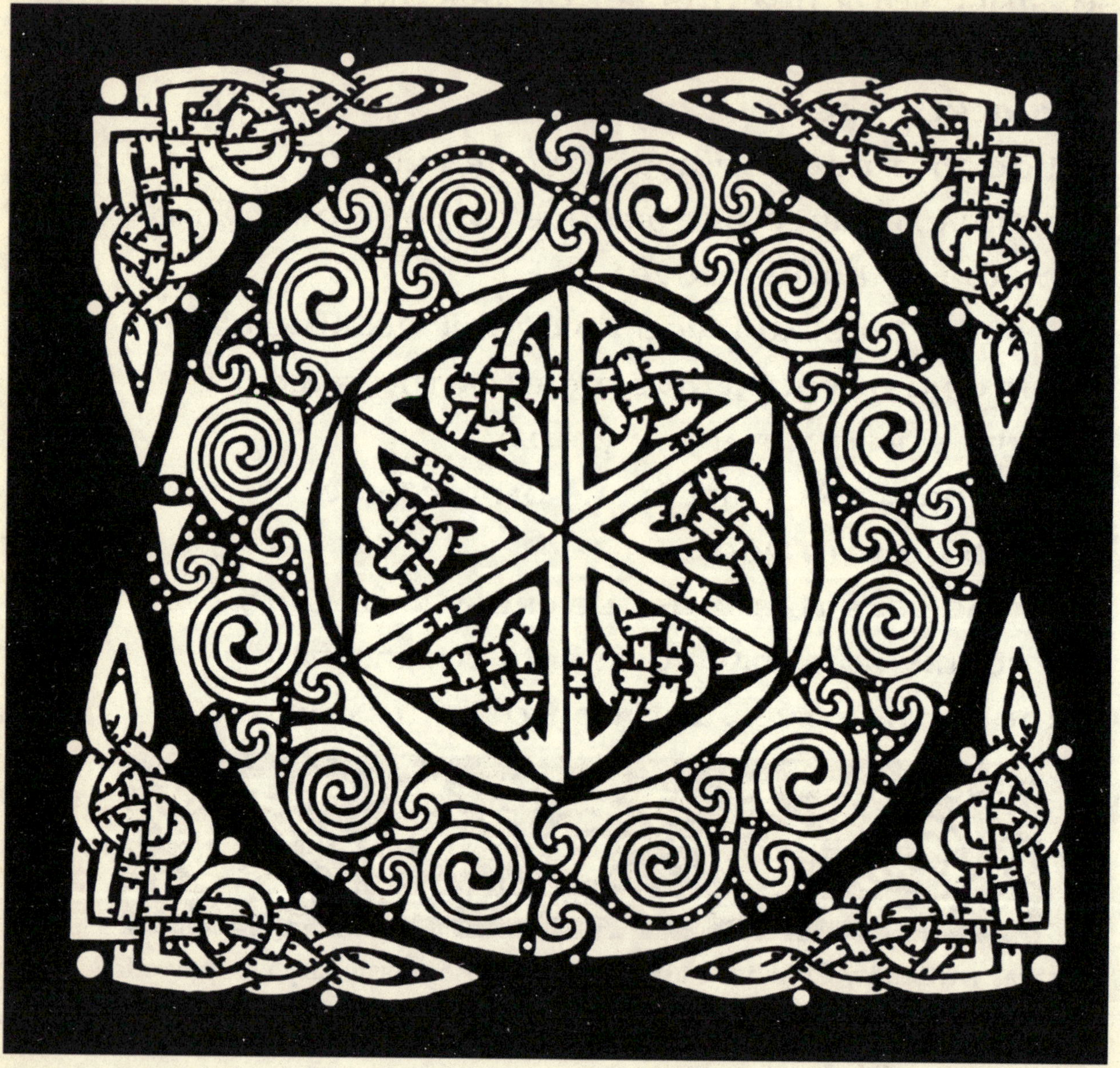

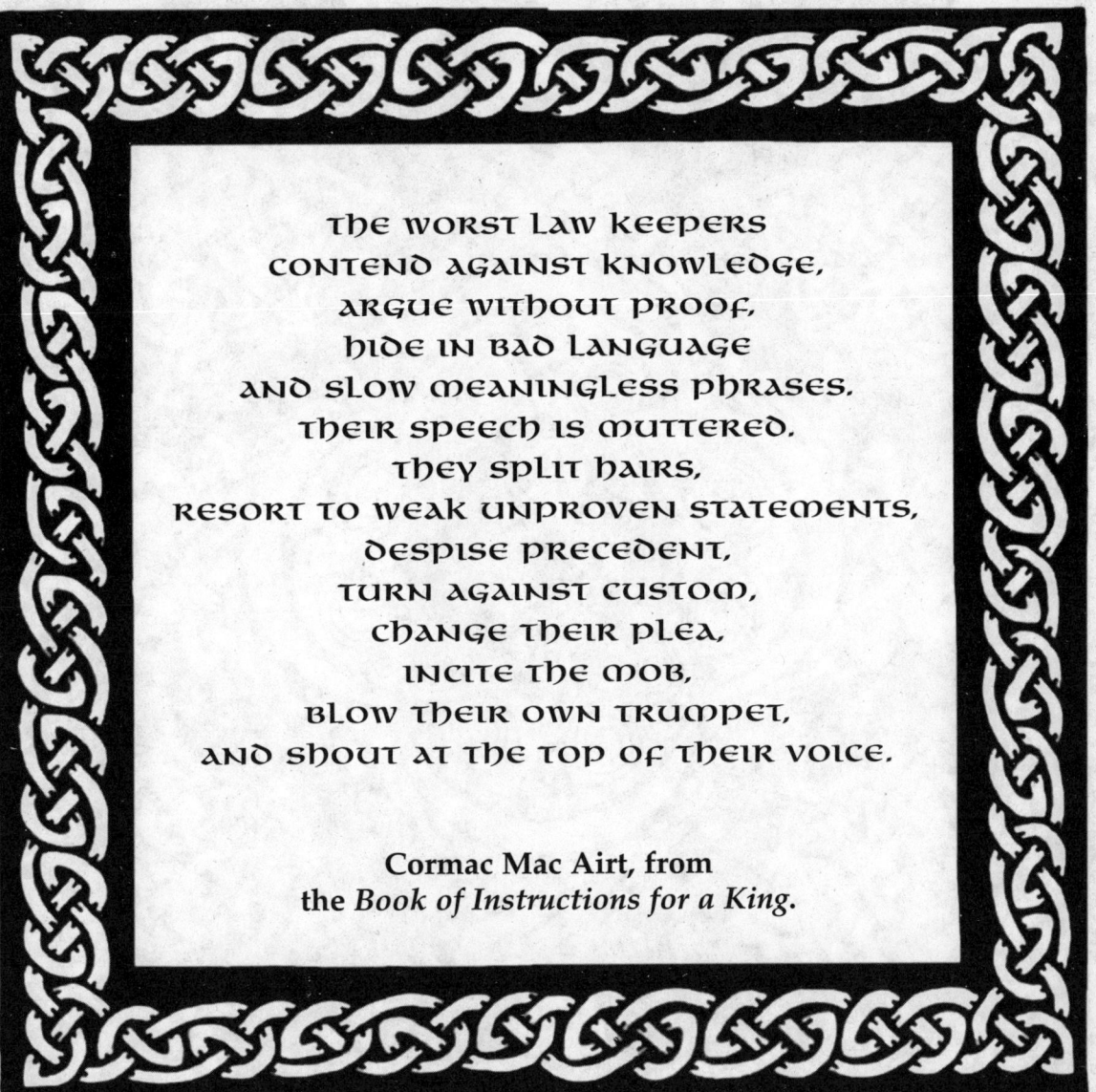

THE WORST LAW KEEPERS
CONTEND AGAINST KNOWLEDGE,
ARGUE WITHOUT PROOF,
HIDE IN BAD LANGUAGE
AND SLOW MEANINGLESS PHRASES.
THEIR SPEECH IS MUTTERED.
THEY SPLIT HAIRS,
RESORT TO WEAK UNPROVEN STATEMENTS,
DESPISE PRECEDENT,
TURN AGAINST CUSTOM,
CHANGE THEIR PLEA,
INCITE THE MOB,
BLOW THEIR OWN TRUMPET,
AND SHOUT AT THE TOP OF THEIR VOICE.

Cormac Mac Airt, from
the *Book of Instructions for a King*.

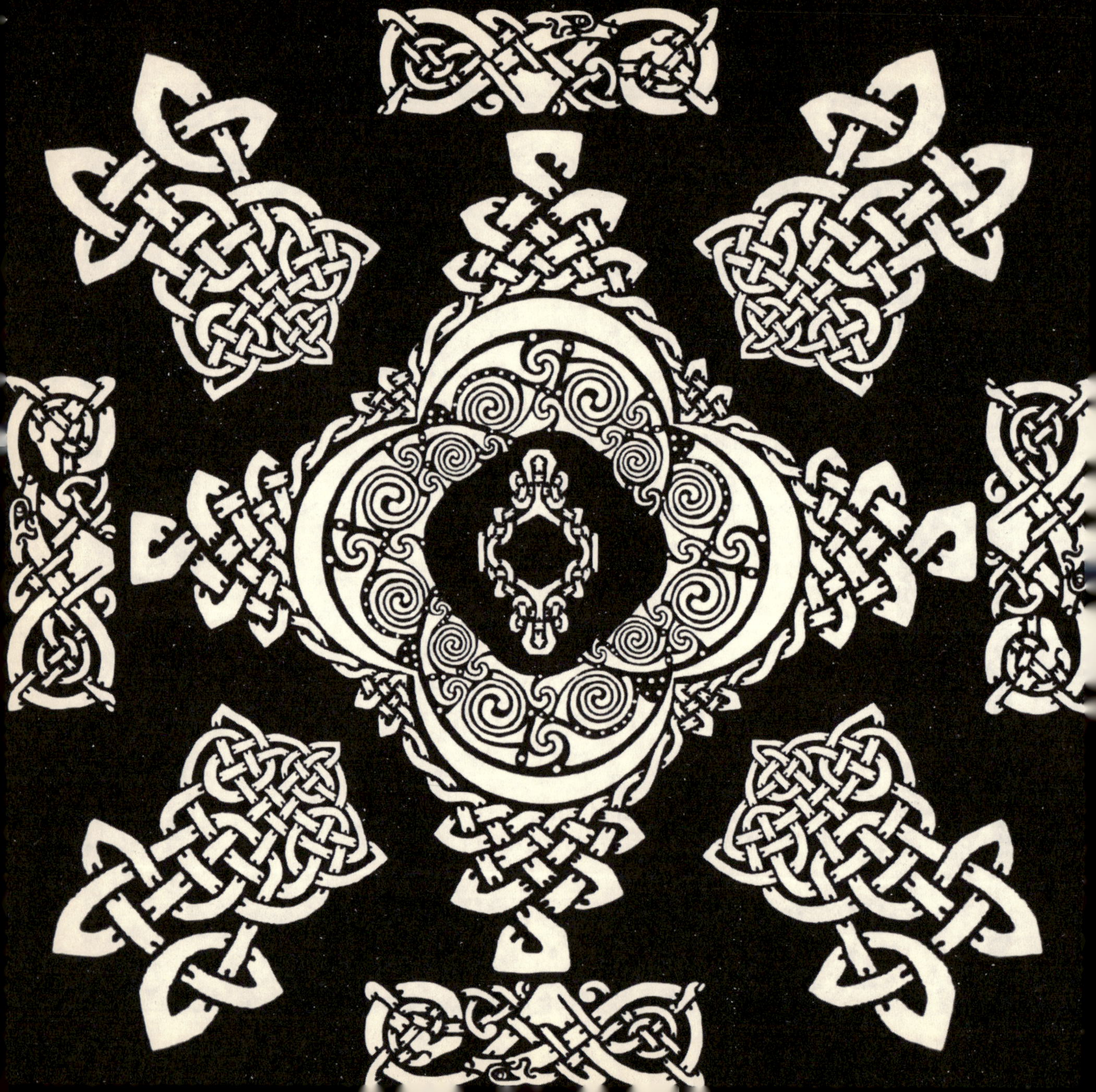

the foot

knows best

where the shoe

pinches

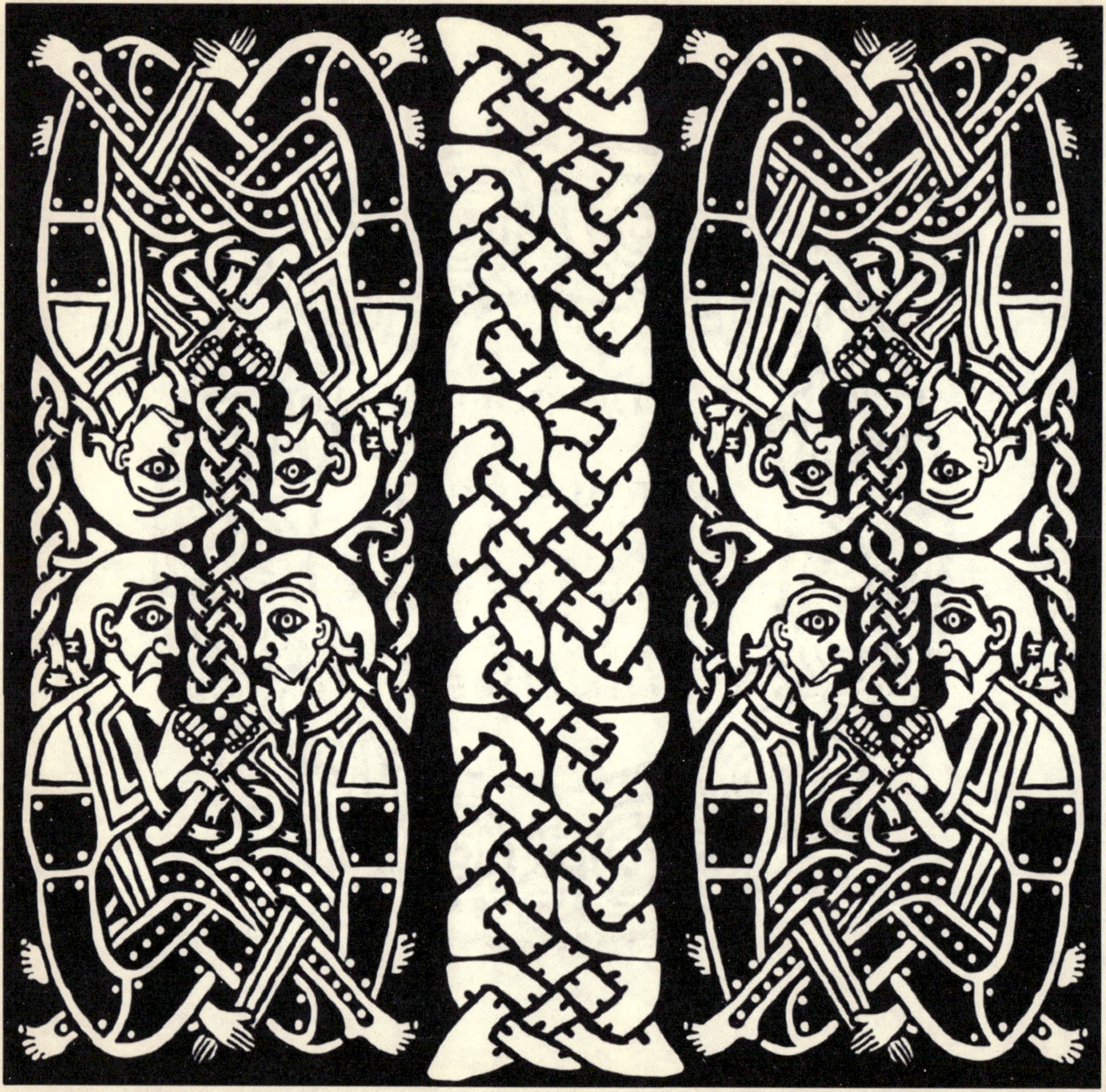

THERE IS NO HUNGER LIKE THE LACK OF A FRIEND

THE THREE STAGES

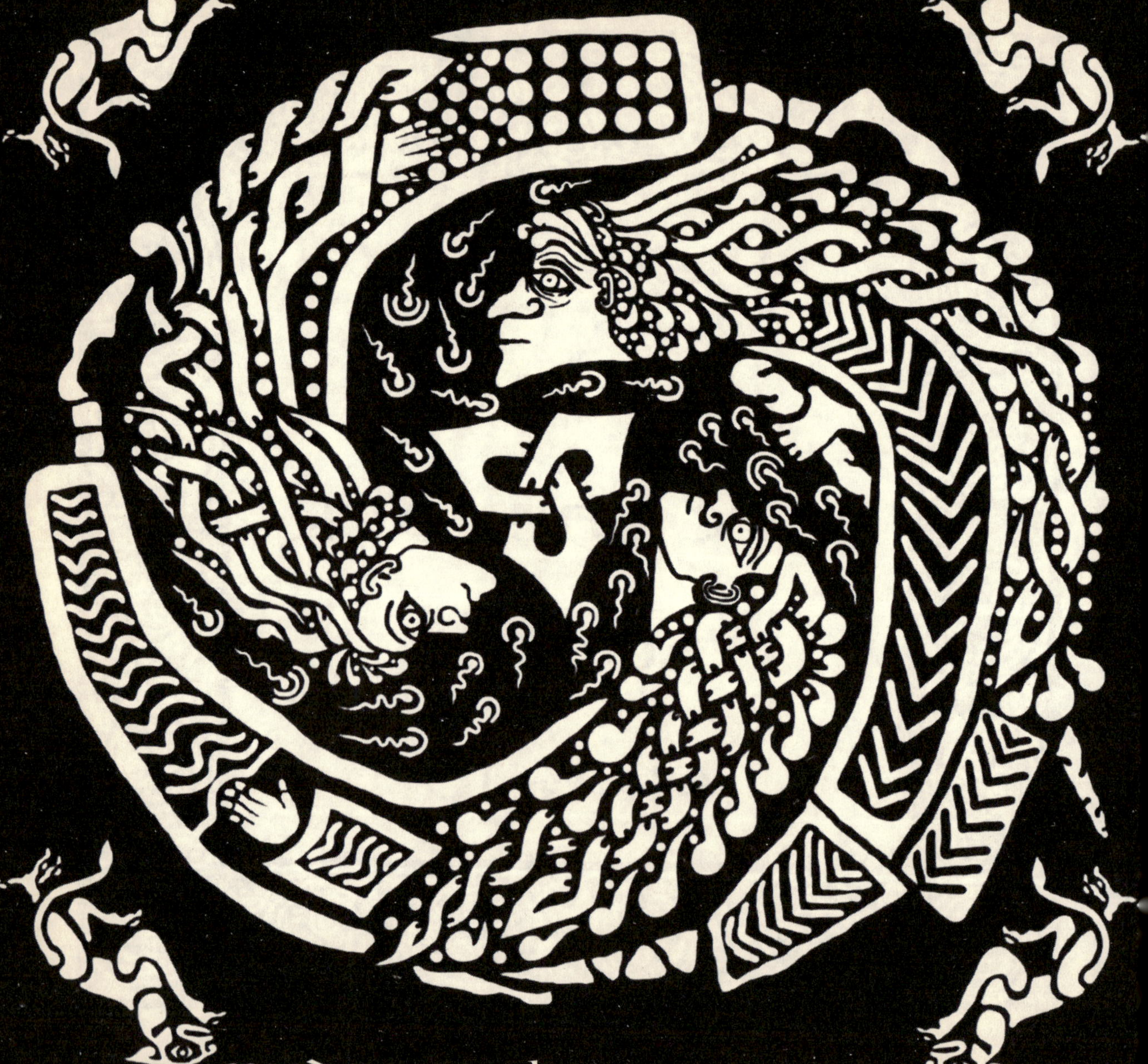

MAIDEN, MOTHER, WISE CRONE

THE THREE STAGES OF LIFE

The ancient Celts believed that life passed through three distinct stages which were celebrated at special rites of passage. Women passed from maiden to mother to wise crone and men from youth to warrior to counsellor. The idea of the Holy Trinity originated with this concept of three people existing within one ageing body. To the Celts the number three embodied all that was sacred and magical.

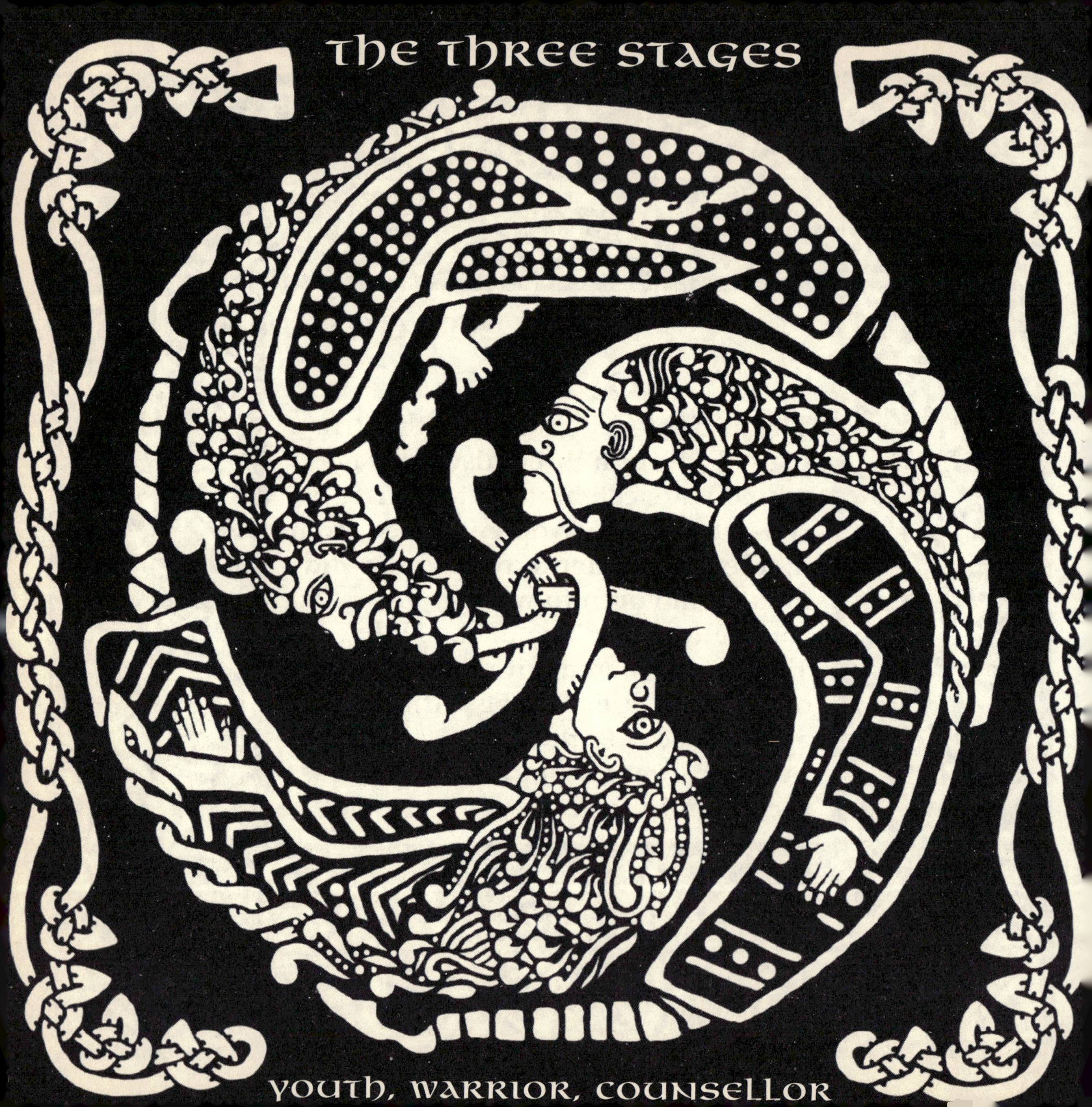
THE THREE STAGES
YOUTH, WARRIOR, COUNSELLOR

ONCE MY HAIR WAS YELLOW-GOLD. NOW

MY HAIR GROWS A SHORT, GREY CROP.

I WOULD RATHER HAVE HAIR THE COLOUR

OF A RAVEN'S WING THAN A SHORT, GREY

CROP.

I NO LONGER COURT WOMEN, THEY DO

NOT LOOK AT ME. MY HAIR IS GREY. I SHALL

NEVER BE AS I WAS.

From a ninth-century manuscript.

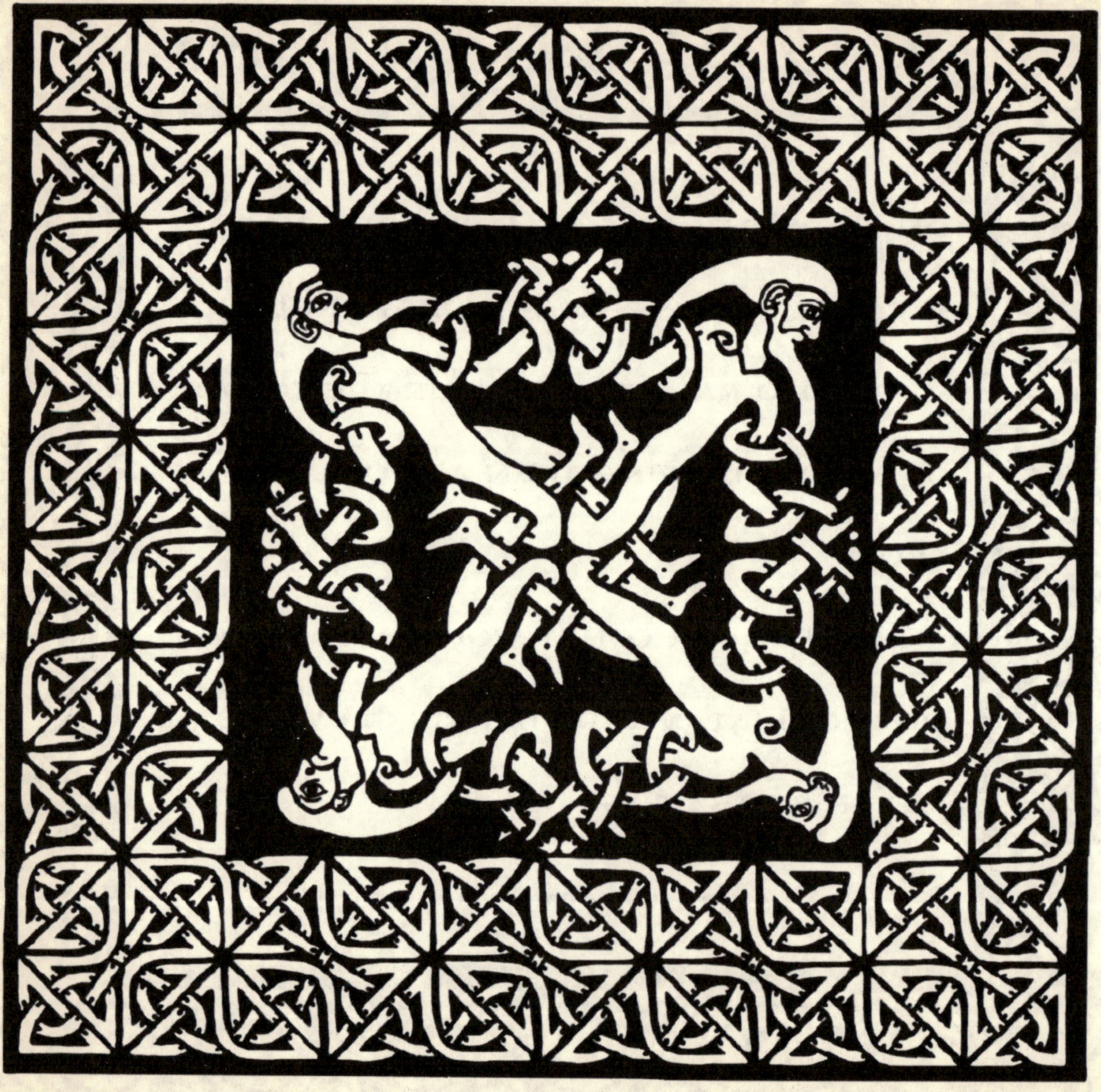

DO NOT
GIVE
A SWORD
TO A MAN
WHO
CANNOT DANCE

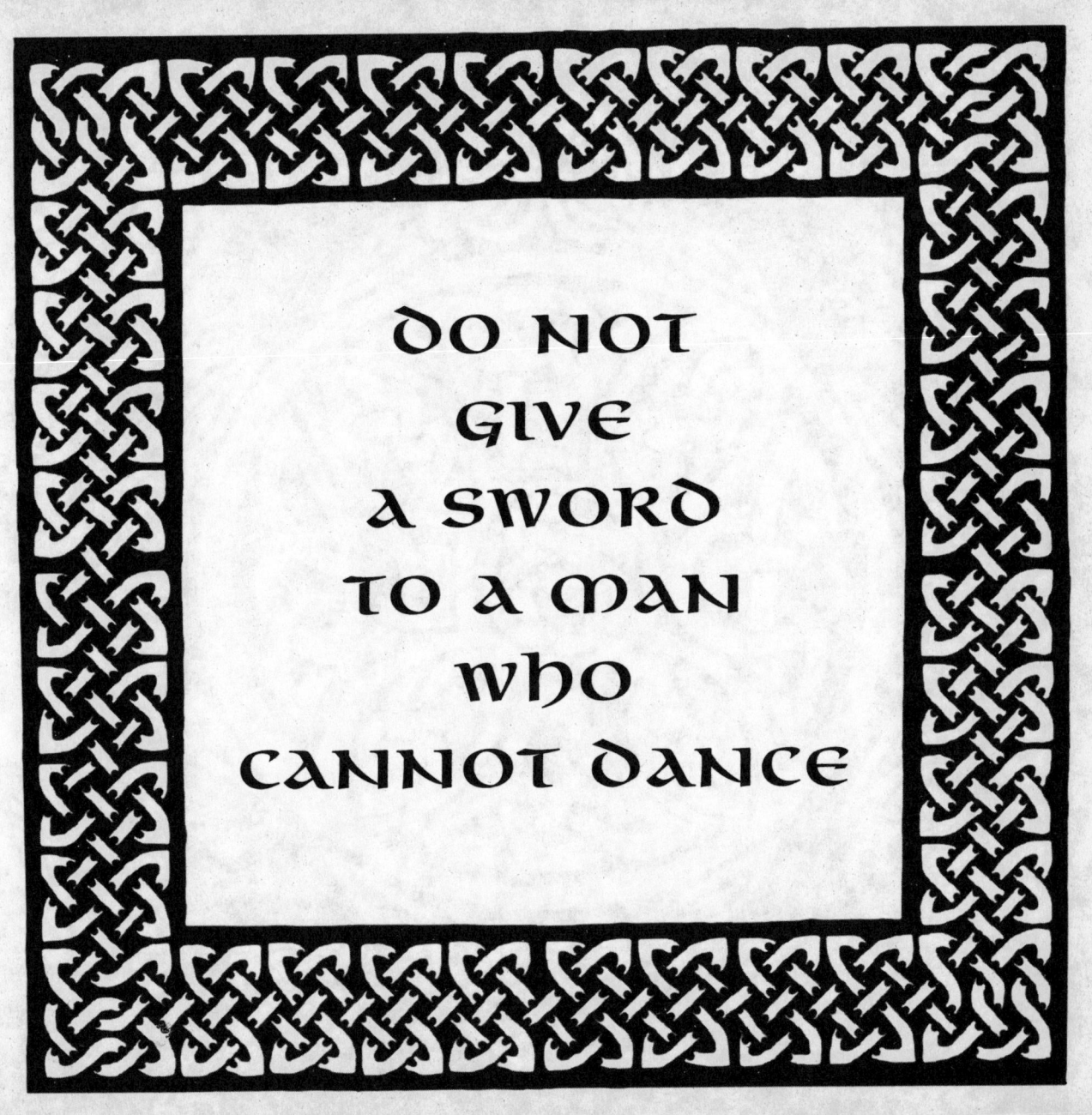

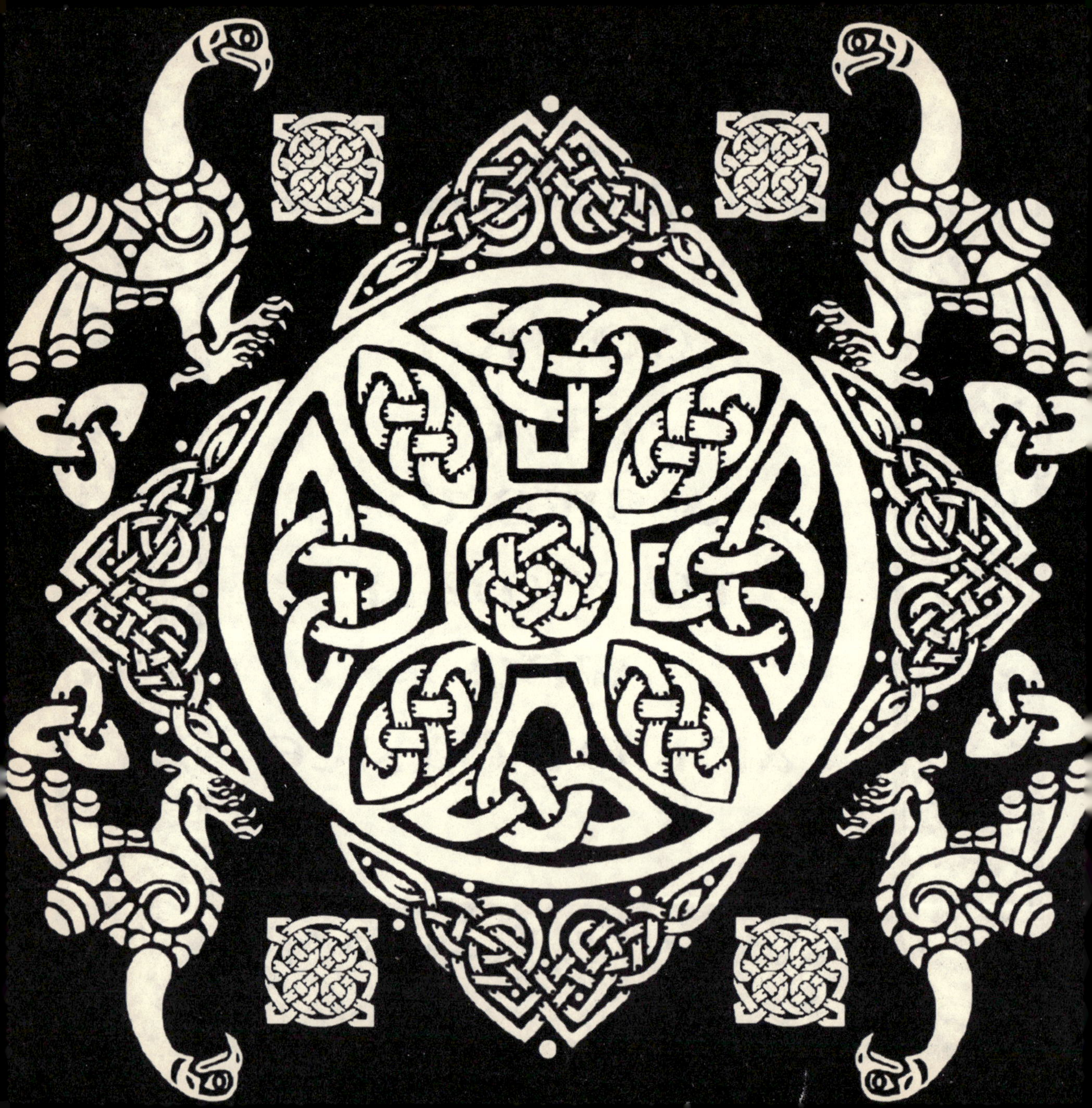

I FEASTED IN THE HALL OF FIONN,

AND AT EACH BANQUET THERE I SAW

A THOUSAND RICH CUPS ON HIS BOARD,

WHOSE RIMS WERE BOUND WITH PUREST GOLD.

AND TWELVE GREAT BUILDINGS ONCE STOOD THERE,

THE DWELLINGS OF THOSE MIGHTY HOSTS,

RULED BY TADG'S WARLIKE SON,

AT ALMA OF THE NOBLE FIAN.

AND CONSTANTLY THERE BURNED TWELVE FIRES,

WITHIN EACH PRINCELY HOUSE OF THESE,

AND ROUND EACH FLAMING HEARTH THERE SAT

A HUNDRED WARRIORS OF THE FIAN.

An anonymous Irish poem written from the point of view of one
of the last of the Fianna.

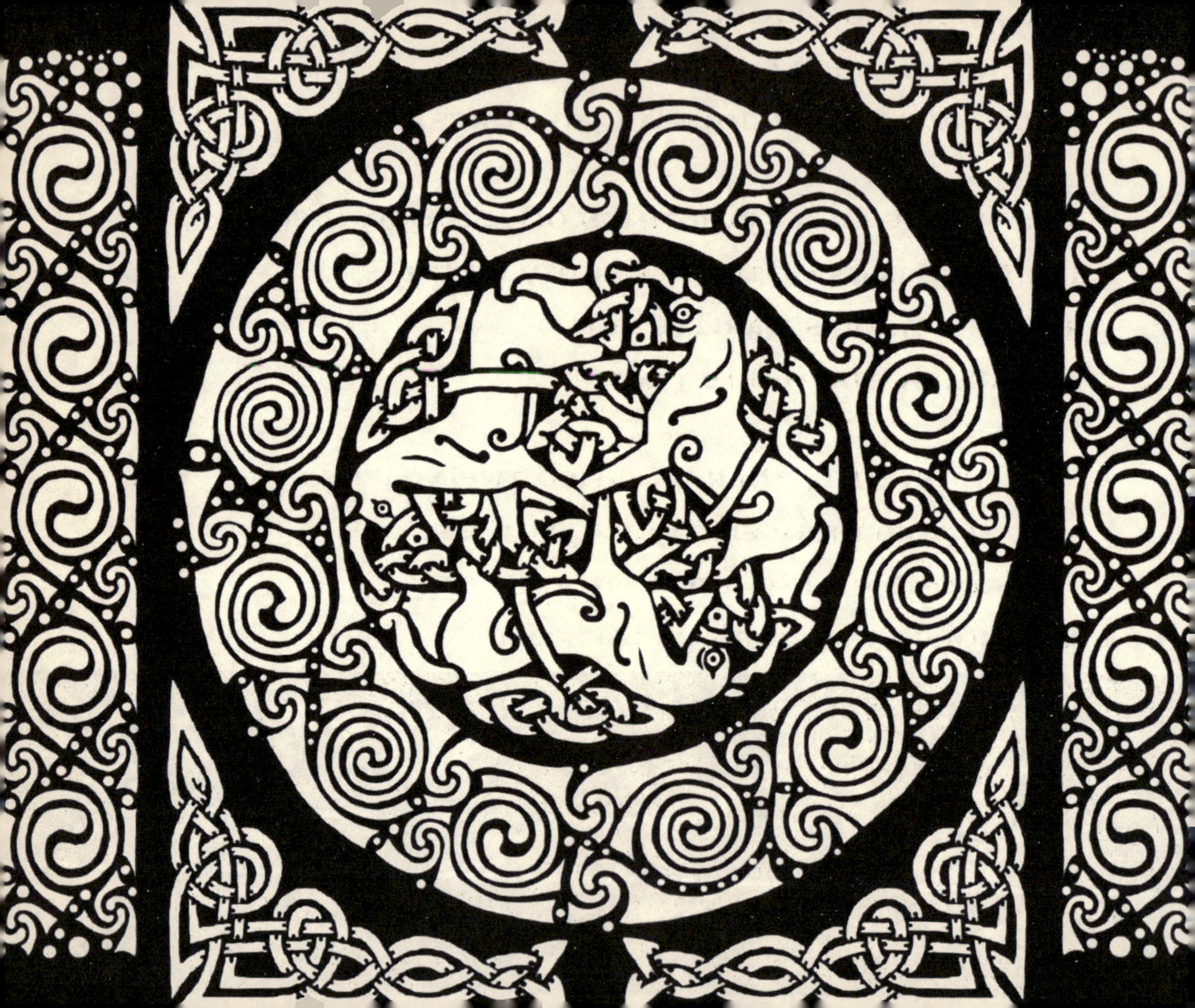

LOVE AND WAR
ARE ALL THE SAME;
MANY A GREAT LOVE
ENDED IN WAR
AND
MANY A GREAT WAR
WAS FOUGHT FOR LOVE.

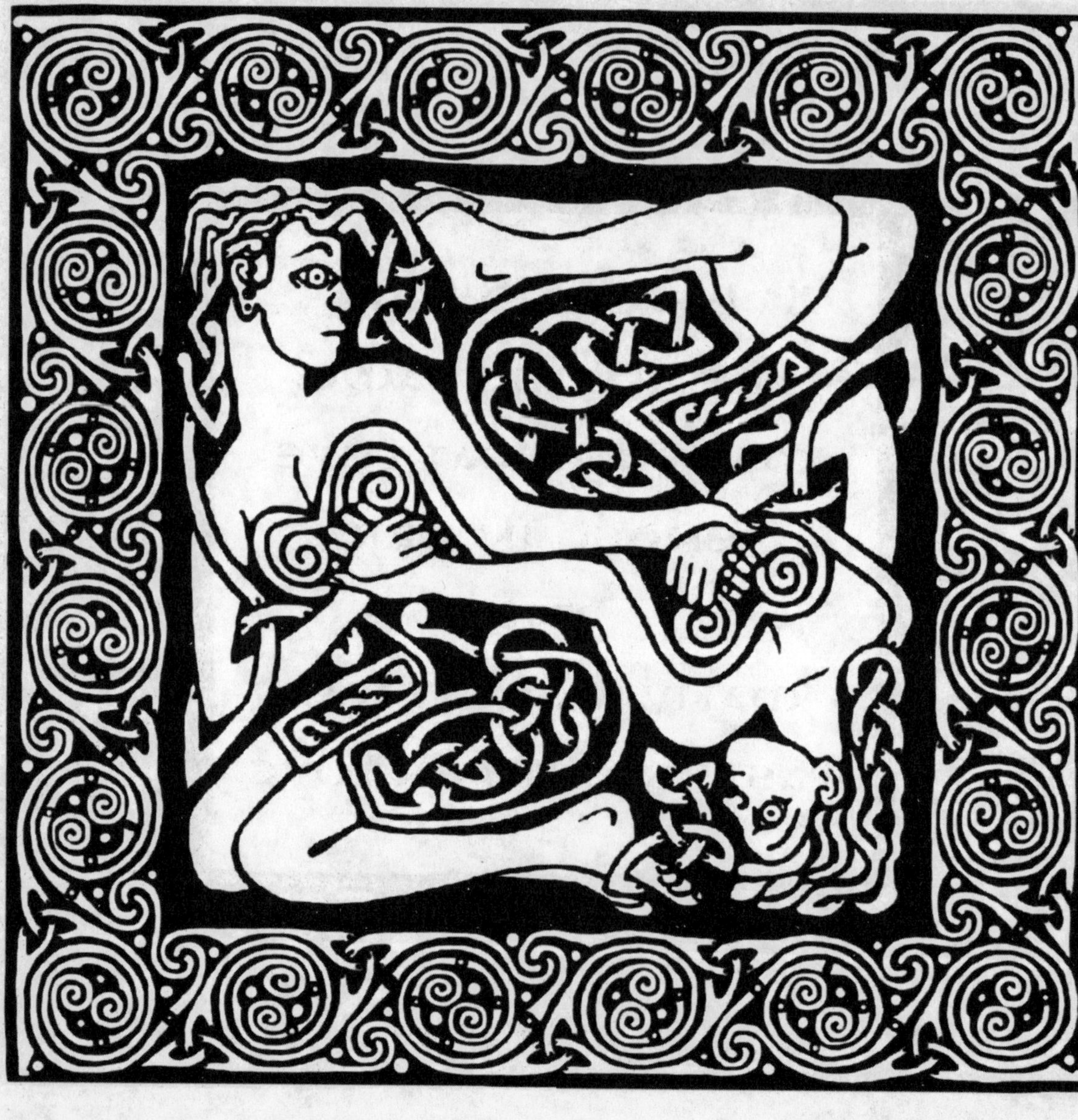

THE EYE OF
A FRIEND
IS THE BEST
MIRROR

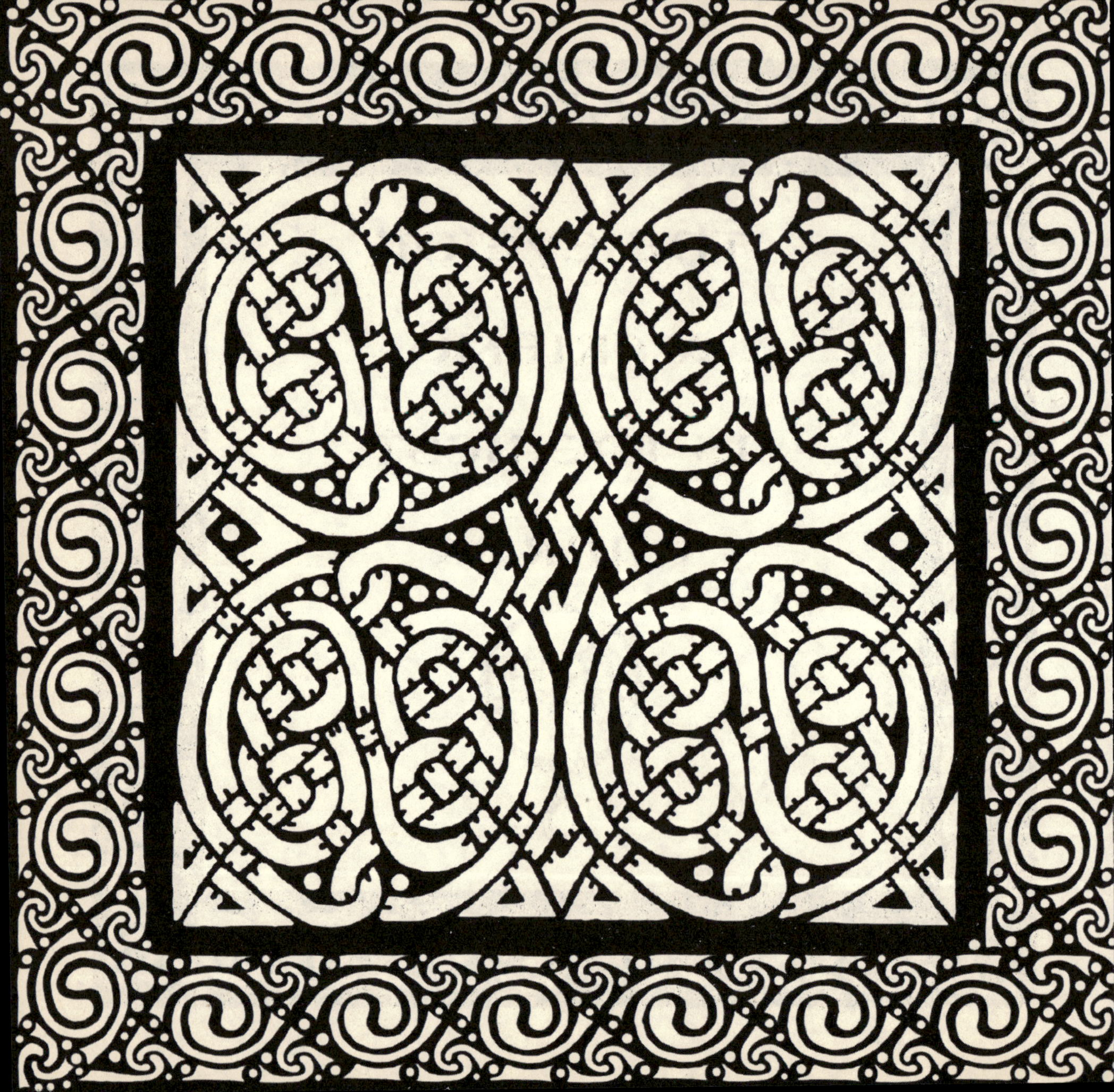

MY GOOD SOUL FRIEND,

MESSENGER OF GOD,

PROTECT MY BODY AND MY SOUL;

PROTECT ME FROM ALL EVIL,

AND ABOVE ALL ELSE FROM SIN.

From a ninth-century manuscript.

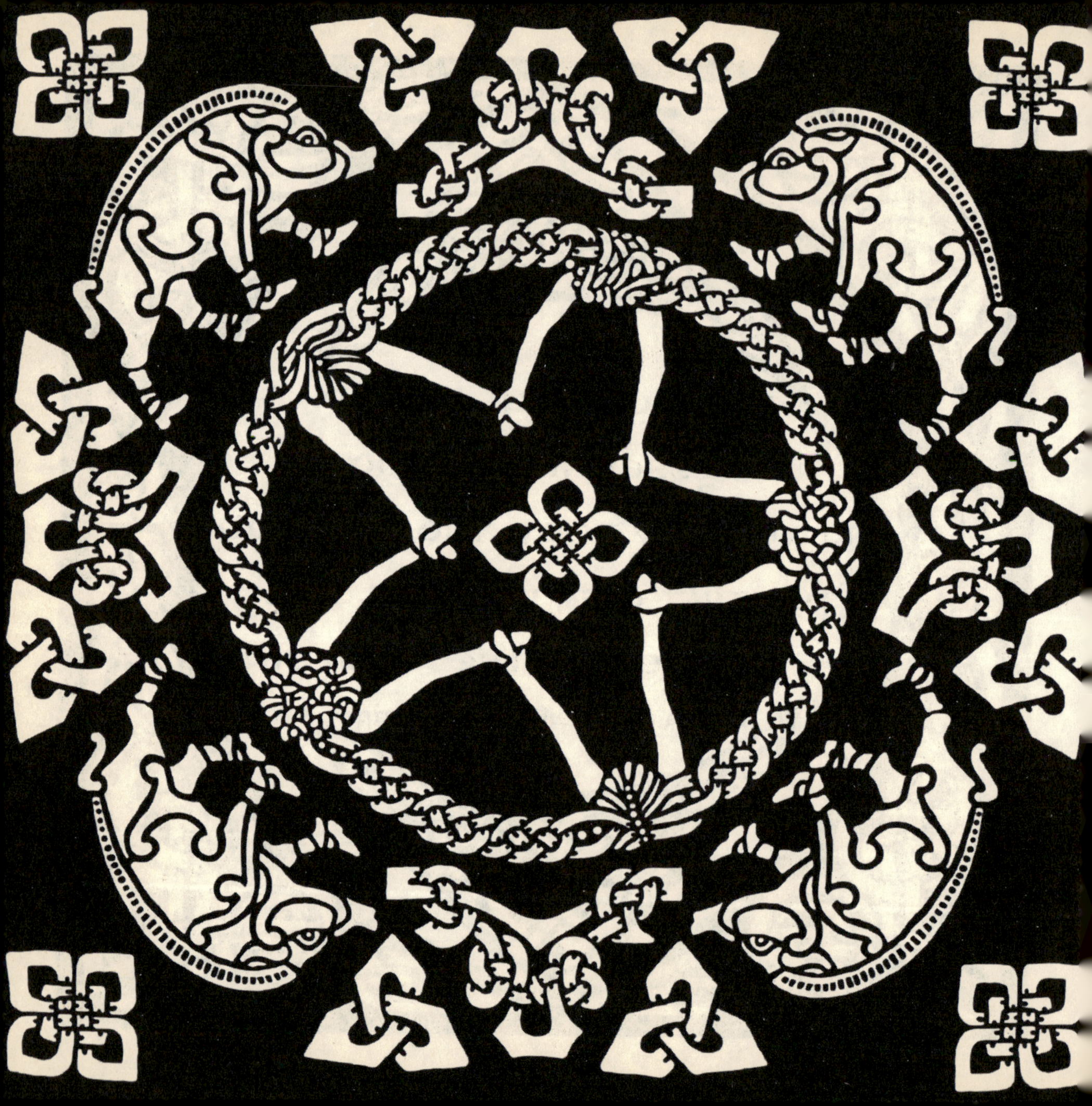

a light heart

lives long

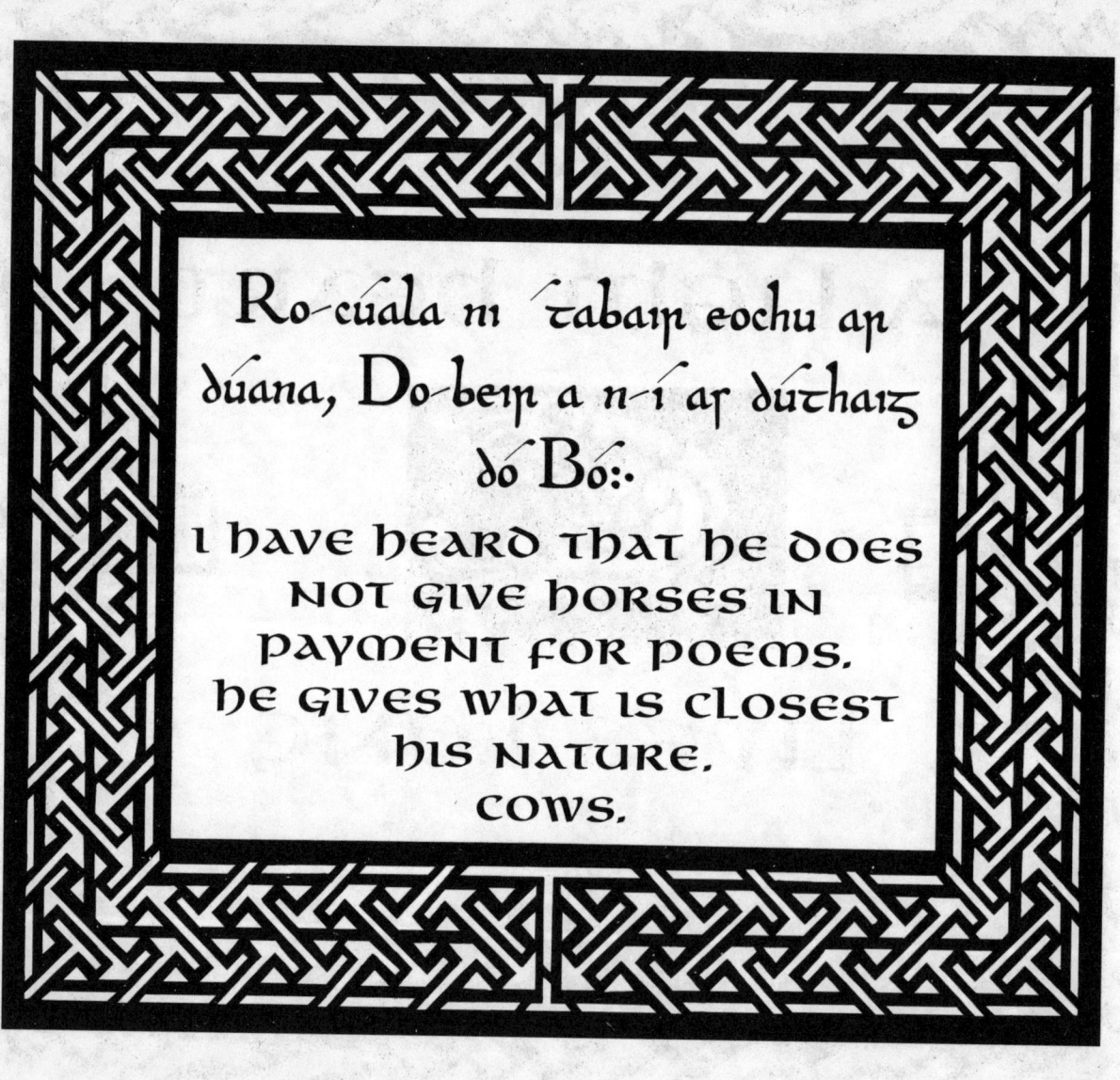

Ro cuala ni tabairp eochu ar
duana, Do berp a n-í ar dúthaig
dó Bó:.

I HAVE HEARD THAT HE DOES
NOT GIVE HORSES IN
PAYMENT FOR POEMS.
HE GIVES WHAT IS CLOSEST
HIS NATURE,
COWS.

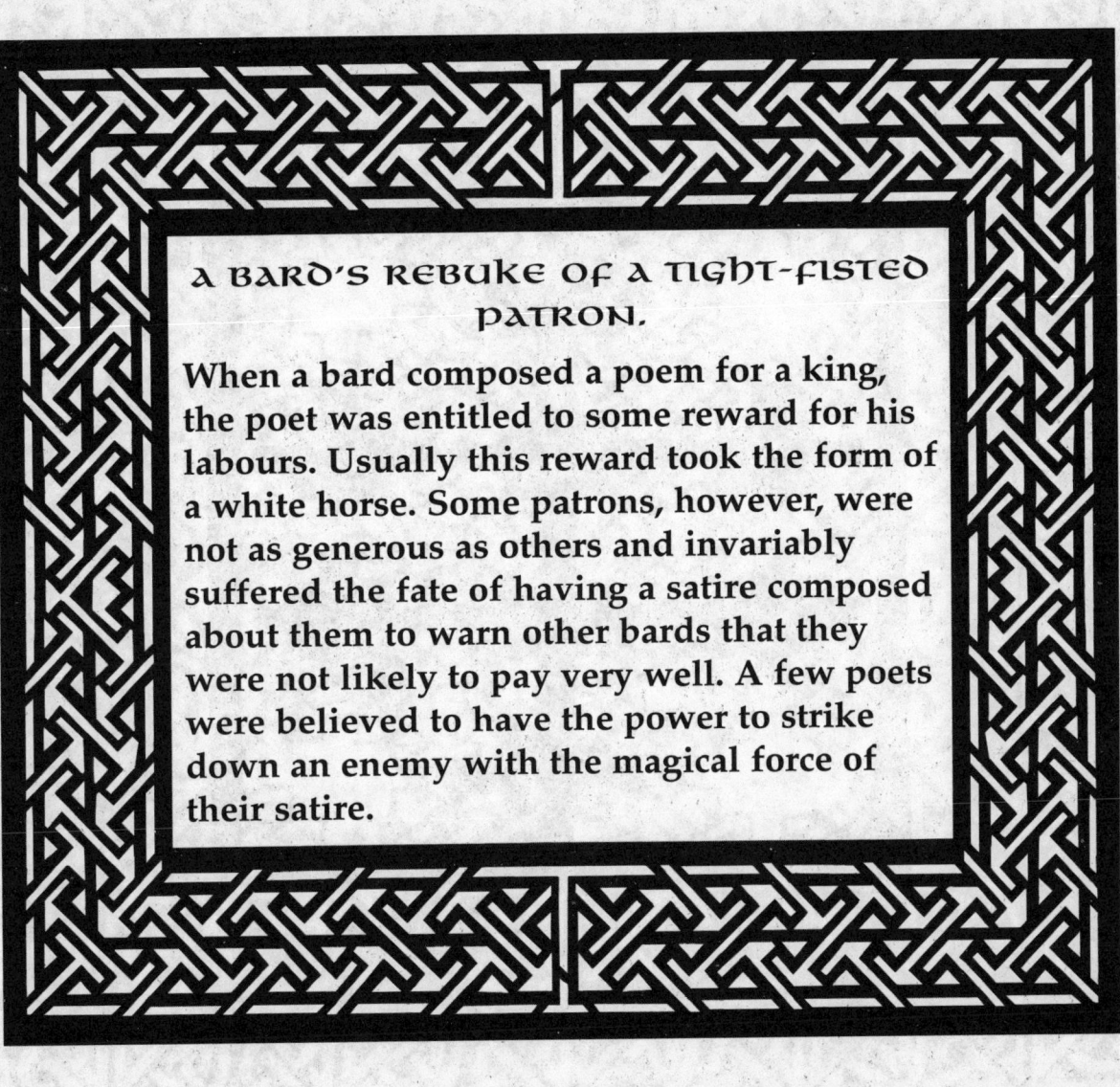

A BARD'S REBUKE OF A TIGHT-FISTED PATRON.

When a bard composed a poem for a king, the poet was entitled to some reward for his labours. Usually this reward took the form of a white horse. Some patrons, however, were not as generous as others and invariably suffered the fate of having a satire composed about them to warn other bards that they were not likely to pay very well. A few poets were believed to have the power to strike down an enemy with the magical force of their satire.

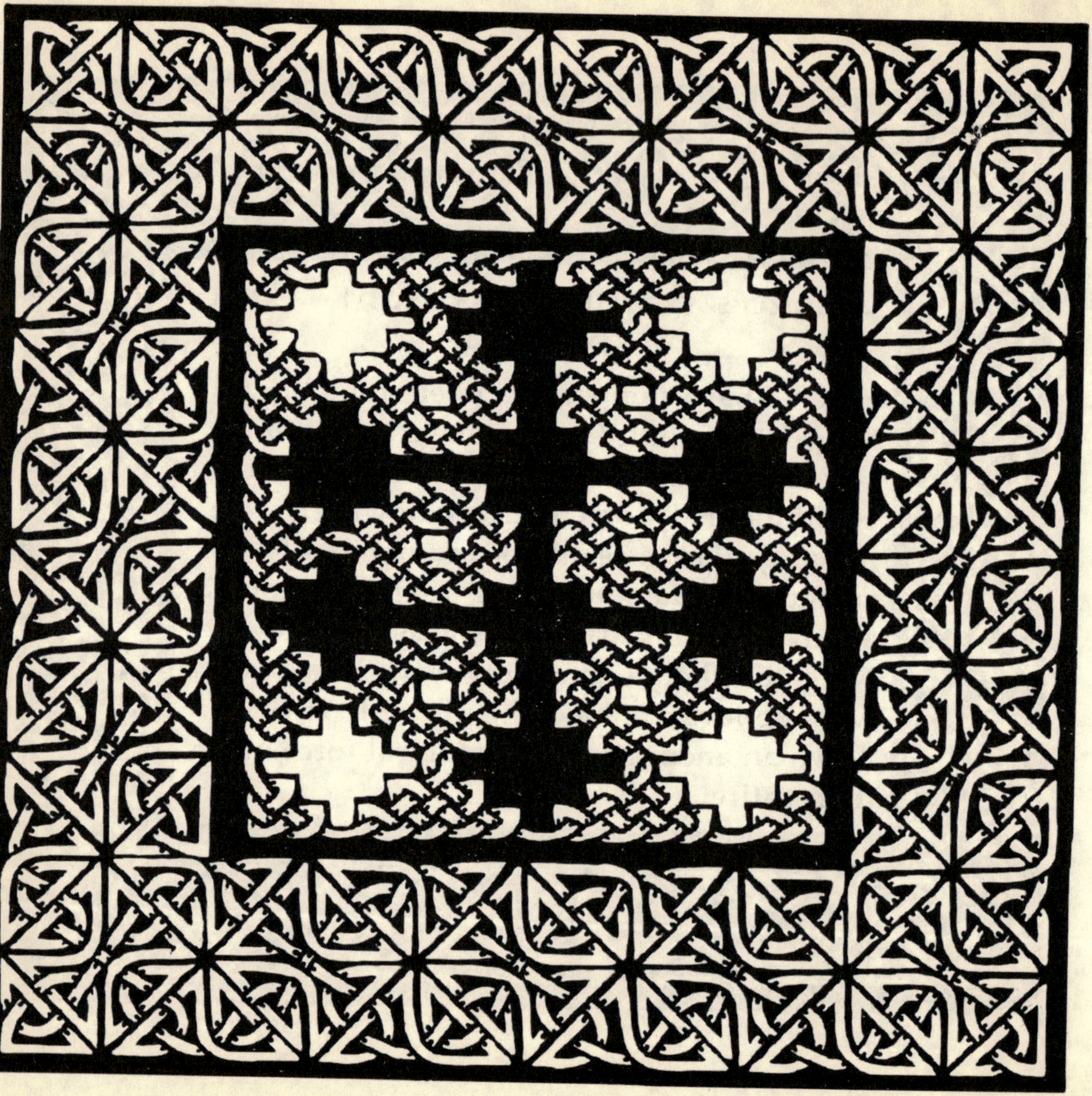

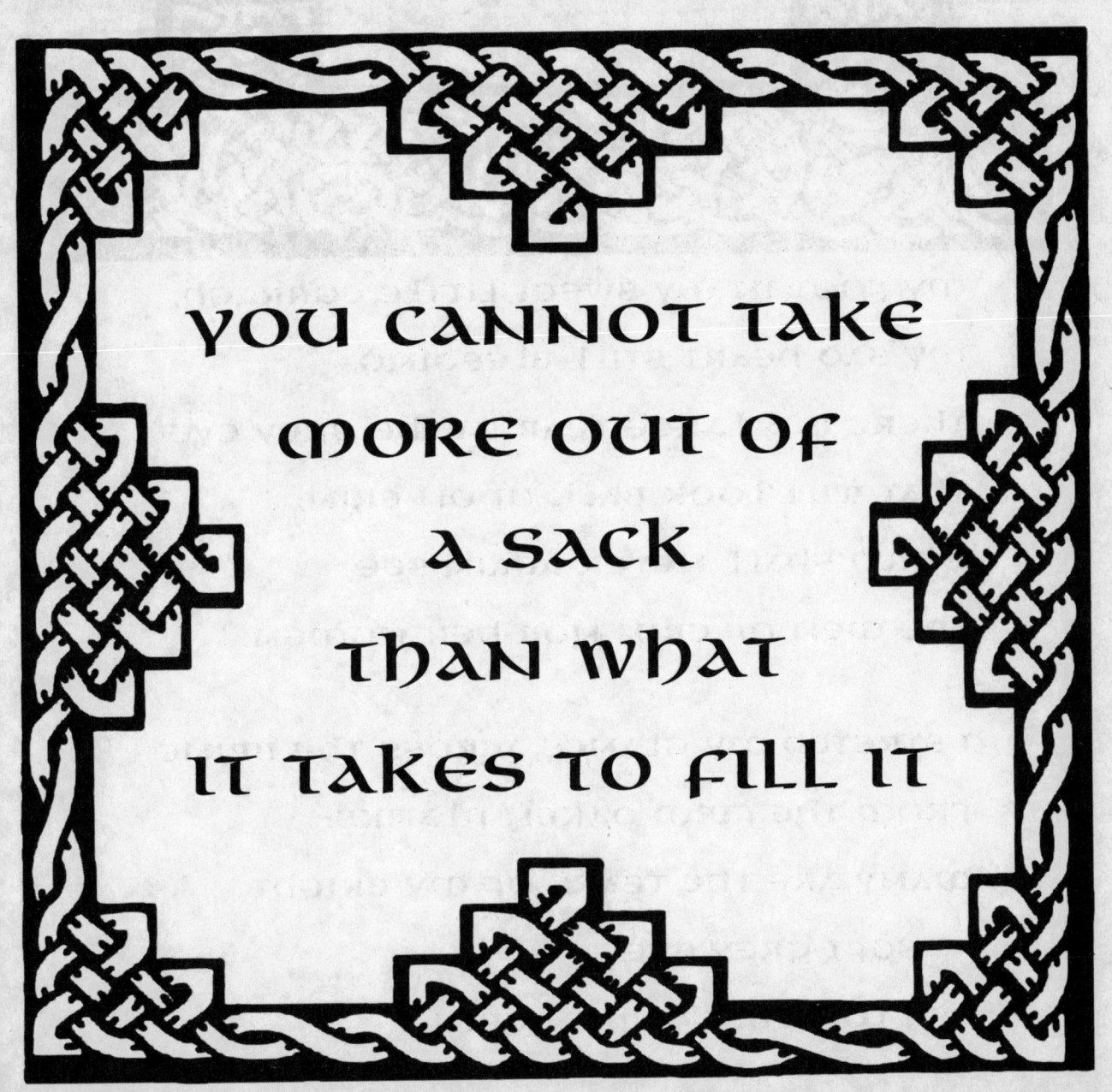

YOU CANNOT TAKE
MORE OUT OF
A SACK
THAN WHAT
IT TAKES TO FILL IT

My foot in my sweet little curragh,

My sad heart still bleeding,

There is a large tear in the grey eye

That will look back upon Erin;

Which shall never again see

The men of Erin nor her women.

I stretch my glance across the brine

From the firm oaken planks;

Many are the tears of my bright

   soft grey eye

As I look back upon Erin.

CARRY, WIND, MY BLESSING

WITH THEE TO THE WEST.

MY HEART IS BROKEN IN MY BREAST;

WERE ALL ALBA MINE

FROM ITS CENTRE TO ITS BORDER,

I WOULD RATHER HAVE A HOUSE

IN THE MIDDLE OF FAIR DERRY.

Colmcille's (Saint Columba's) lament for Eirinn. This saint was caught copying a manuscript without the permission of its owner. The High-King was brought in to mediate in the resulting dispute. He made the famous judgement that when a cow bears a calf, the offspring belongs to the farmer who owns the cow, so when a book is copied the new book belongs to the owner of the original manuscript. Colmcille refused to accept the judgement, raised an army and began a bloody war over the book. His soldiers were eventually defeated and he was exiled to Scotland, known in those times as Alba.

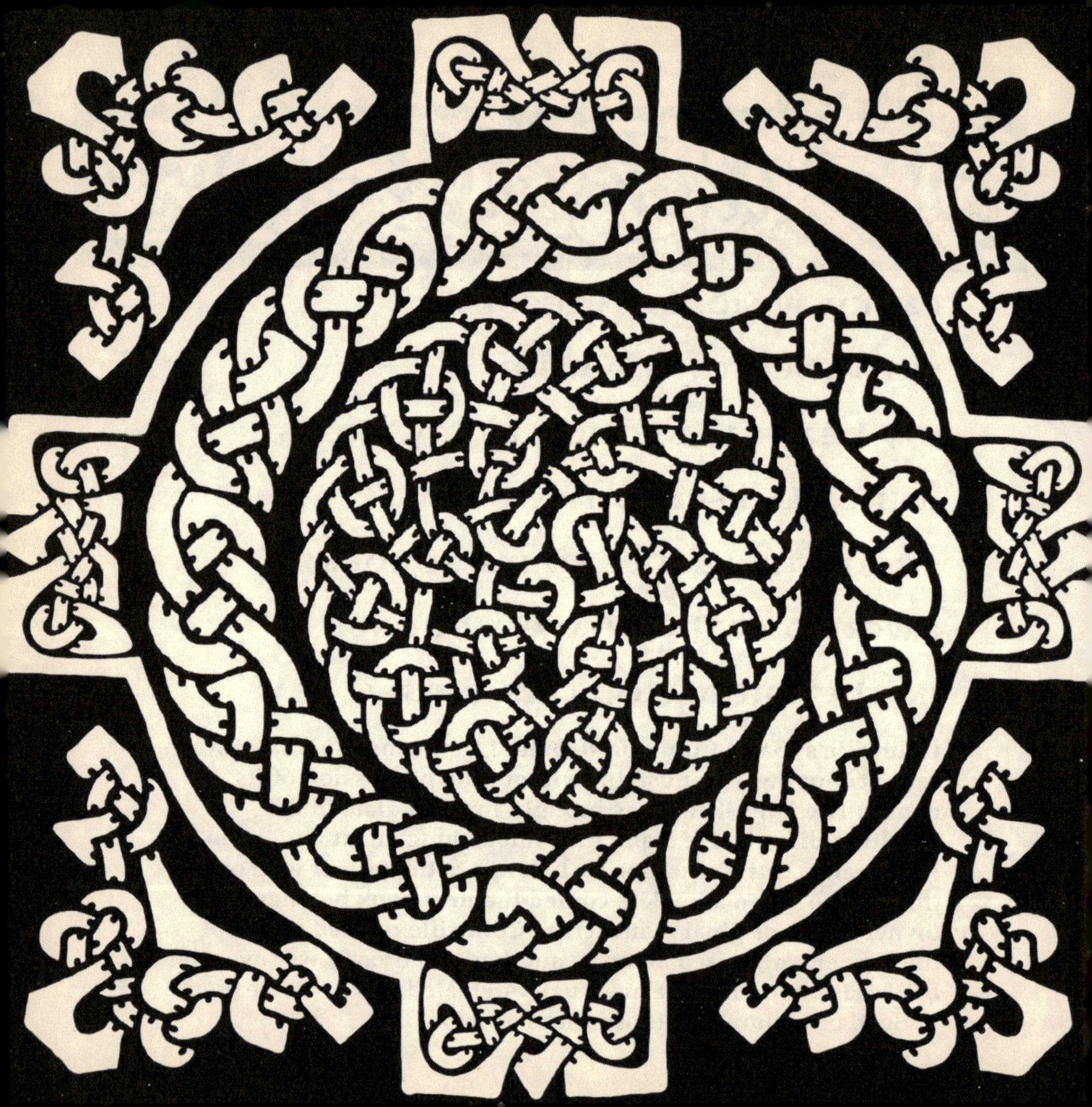

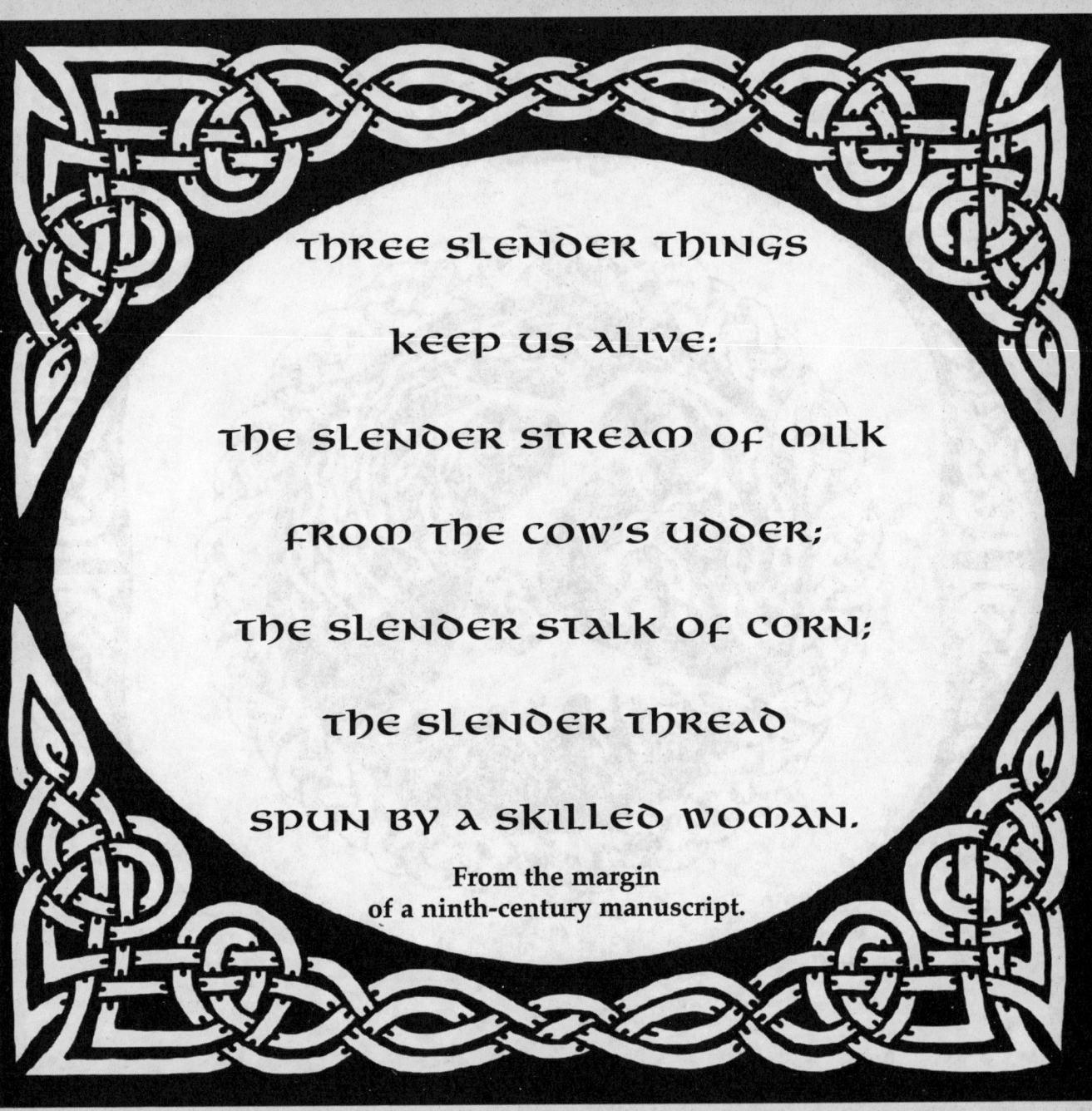

THREE SLENDER THINGS

KEEP US ALIVE:

THE SLENDER STREAM OF MILK

FROM THE COW'S UDDER;

THE SLENDER STALK OF CORN;

THE SLENDER THREAD

SPUN BY A SKILLED WOMAN.

From the margin
of a ninth-century manuscript.

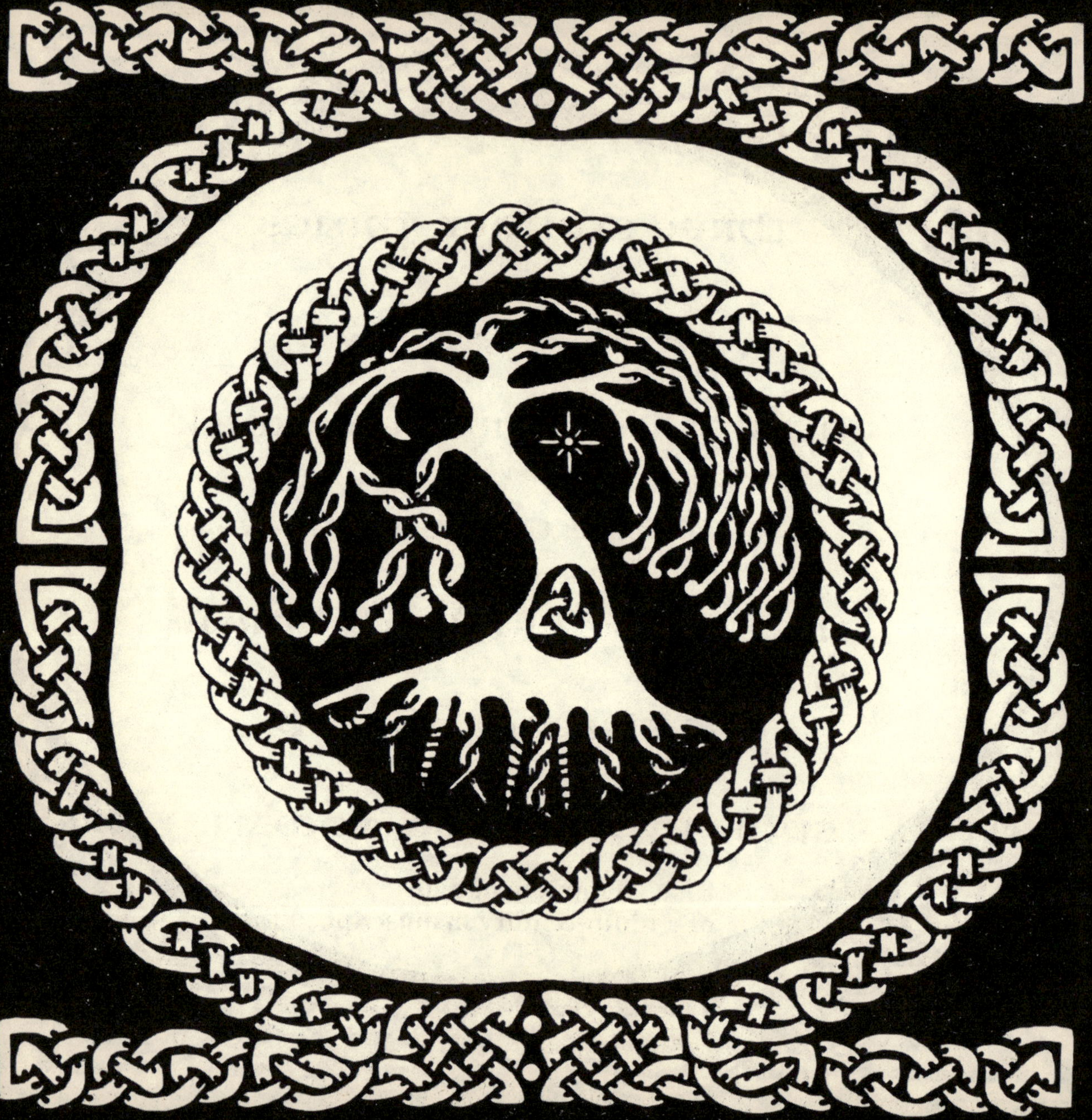

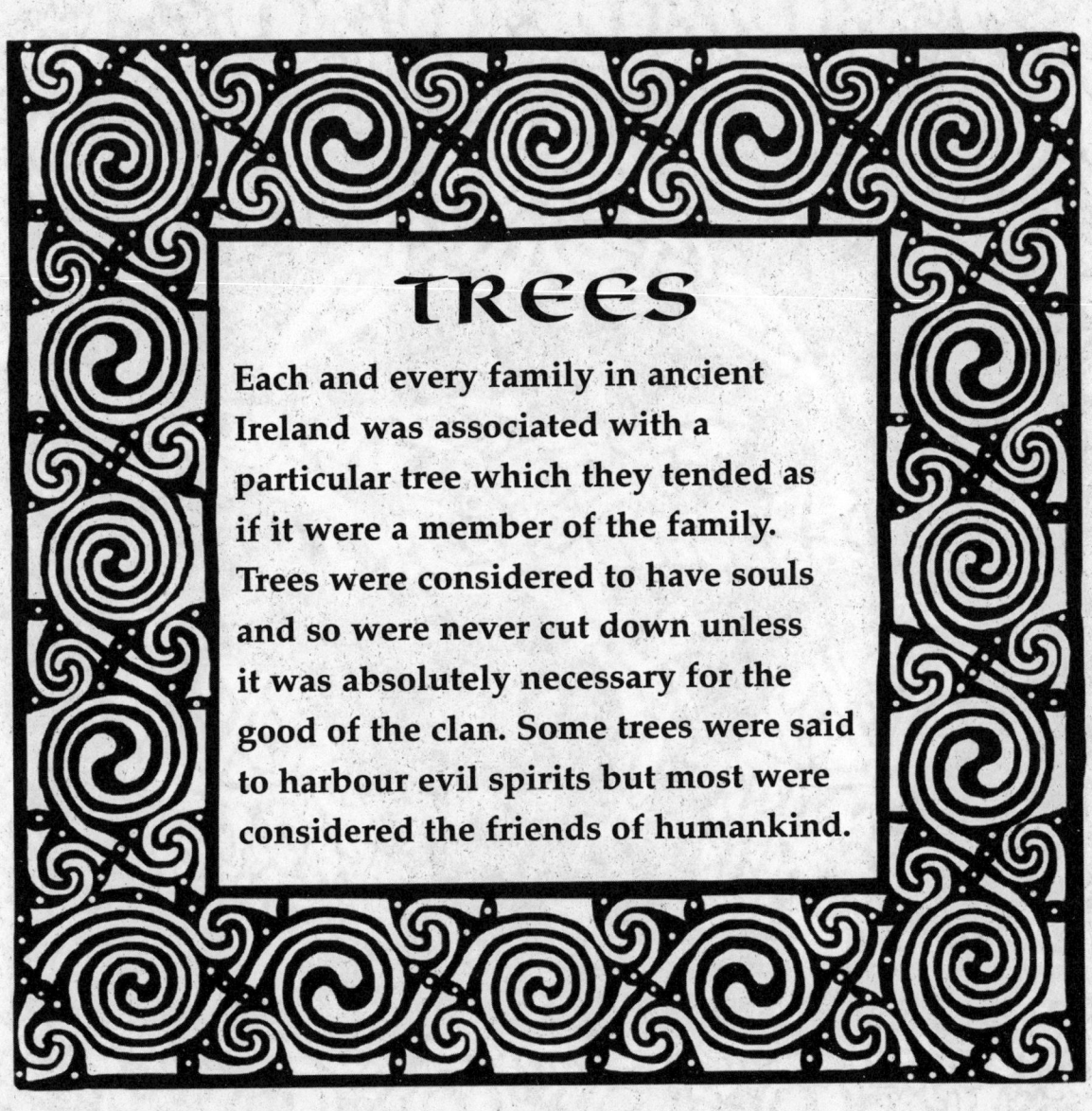

TREES

Each and every family in ancient Ireland was associated with a particular tree which they tended as if it were a member of the family. Trees were considered to have souls and so were never cut down unless it was absolutely necessary for the good of the clan. Some trees were said to harbour evil spirits but most were considered the friends of humankind.

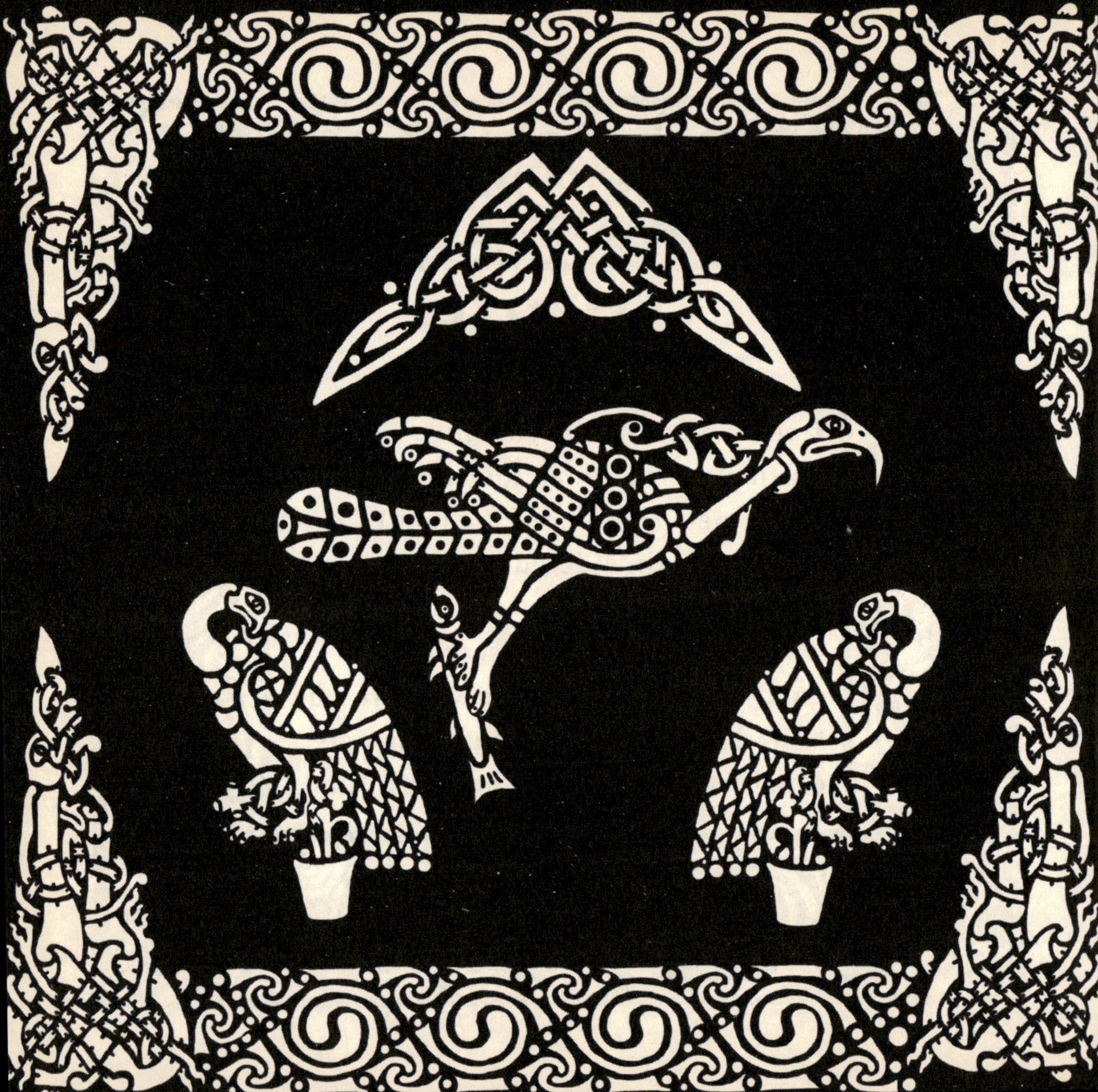

ONLY A FOOL WOULD FAIL

TO PRAISE GOD

IN HIS MIGHT,

WHEN THE TINY,

MINDLESS BIRDS

PRAISE HIM IN THEIR FLIGHT.

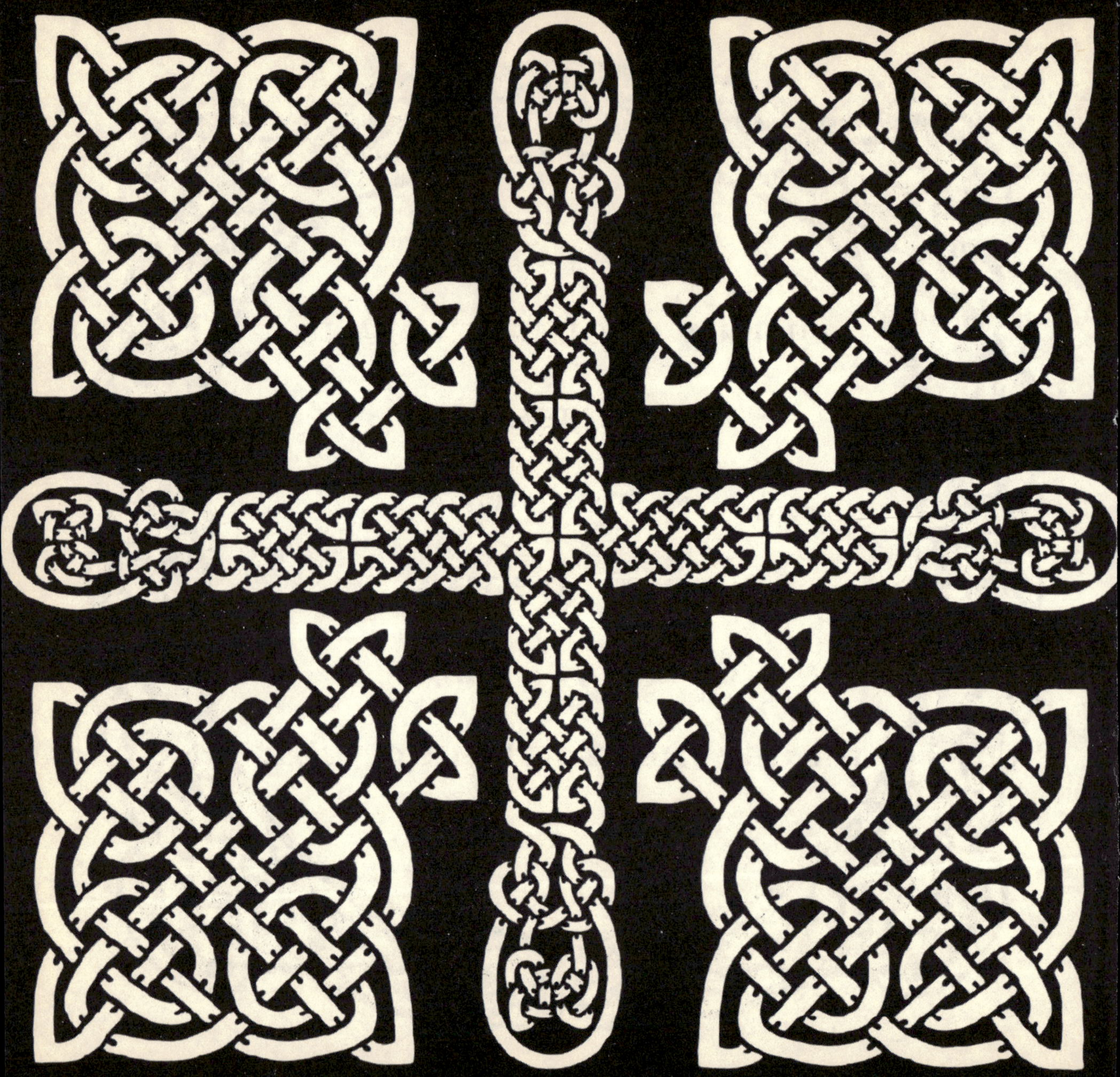

EVERYONE CAN BE

PLEASANT

UNTIL A COW

INVADES THEIR

GARDEN

PRONUNCIATION GUIDE

Amairgen	am-ar-geen
Brandubh	bran-doov
Cailleach	kayl-ack
Cairbre	ko-bray
Colmcille	kolum-kil
Fianna	fee-an-ah
Fionn MacCumhal	finn-mac-coo-hil
Grian	gree-ann
Leabhar Teagasc an Riogh	lev-ar tay-gas un ree
Morrigán	mo-ree-garn
Ogham	ohh-um
Tagd	teeg
Tuatha-De-Danaan	too-ah-ha day-dah-nan